HIGH DESERT BLOOD

HIGH DESERT BLOOD

The 1980 New Mexico Prison Riot
and the Tragedy of the Williams Brothers

Andrew Brininstool

University of Iowa Press, Iowa City

University of Iowa Press, Iowa City 52242
Copyright © 2025 by the University of Iowa Press
uipress.uiowa.edu
Printed in the United States of America

Cover Design by Brad Norr
Text Design and Typesetting by Ashley Muehlbauer

Printed on acid-free paper

Library of Congress Cataloging-in-Publication Data

Names: Brininstool, Andrew, author.
Title: High Desert Blood: The 1980 New Mexico Prison Riot
and the Tragedy of the Williams Brothers / Andrew Brininstool.
Description: Iowa City: University of Iowa Press, [2025]
Identifiers: LCCN 2024046696 (print) | LCCN 2024046697
(ebook) | ISBN 9781609389697 (paperback) |
ISBN 9781609389703 (ebook)
Subjects: LCSH: Prison riots—New Mexico—History—20th
century. | New Mexico State Penitentiary—History.
Classification: LCC HV9475.N62 B75 2025 (print) | LCC HV9475
.N62 (ebook) | DDC 365/.641—dc23/eng/20250130
LC record available at https://lccn.loc.gov/2024046696
LC ebook record available at https://lccn.loc.gov/2024046697

For Janell Whitlock, and for my family

CAST OF CHARACTERS

Carlsbad, New Mexico

A. W. "Dubb" Williams, father of Gary and Jeff
LaDon Garrett Williams, mother of Gary and Jeff
Gary Dru Williams, older brother to Jeffrey Lloyd Williams
Jeffrey Lloyd Williams, younger brother to Gary Dru Williams
Roger Jenkins, friend and business associate to Dubb Williams
Dick Blenden, longtime defense attorney for the Williamses
Tom Cherryhomes, longtime defense attorney, notably for Jeffrey Lloyd
    Williams

Administrators of the penitentiary at the time of the riot

Bruce King, governor
Jeff Bingaman, attorney general
Jerry Griffin, warden
Robert Montoya, deputy warden
Felix Rodriguez, deputy corrections secretary
Manuel Koroneos, superintendent of correctional security
Marc Orner, prison psychologist

Notable postriot defense attorneys

Garvin Isaacs
Mark Donatelli

Notable prison staff on duty during the riot

Captain Gregorio "Greg" Roybal
Lieutenant Jose Anaya
Marcella Armijo, correctional officer meant to be on duty but did not
    show
Carlos Martinez, National Guard sergeant, and among the first inside
    the penitentiary postriot

Notable inmate leaders and victims

Michael Colby

William Jack "Two Pack" Stephens, leader(s) of burgeoning Anglo clique, charged with multiple riot-related homicides

Michael Price, enforcer of burgeoning Anglo clique

Darrell Jean Stelly, enforcer of burgeoning Anglo clique, later to turn state's witness

Bert Duane Stevens, inmate and murder victim, death a catalyst for the rise of the burgeoning Anglo clique

Danny Ray Macias, instigator of the riot's first hours

Lonnie Duran and Kendrick Duran, inmate negotiators

Vincent Candelaria

(later) Dwight Duran

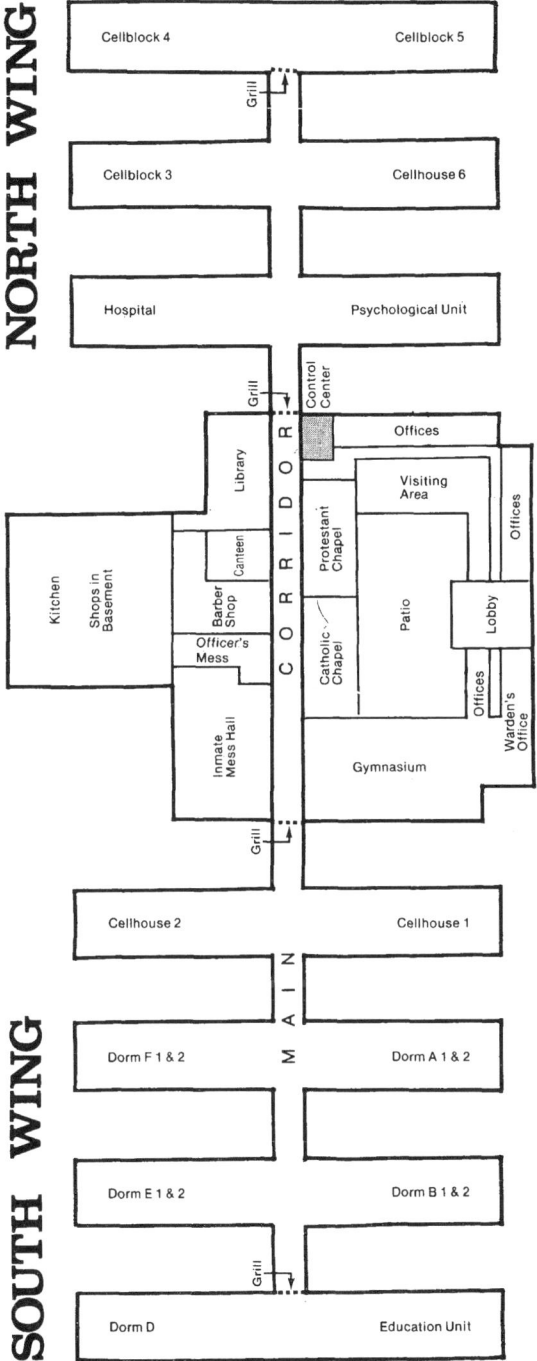

NORTH WING

Cellblock 4   Cellblock 5

Grill

Cellblock 3   Cellhouse 6

Hospital   Psychological Unit

ADMIN AREA

Grill

CORRIDOR

Control Center

Offices

Library

Kitchen

Shops in Basement

Canteen

Barber Shop

Visiting Area

Offices

Protestant Chapel

Officer's Mess

Catholic Chapel

Patio

Lobby

Inmate Mess Hall

Offices

Warden's Office

Gymnasium

Grill

Cellhouse 2   Cellhouse 1

MAIN

Dorm F 1 & 2   Dorm A 1 & 2

Dorm E 1 & 2   Dorm B 1 & 2

Grill

Dorm D   Education Unit

SOUTH WING

THE PENITENTIARY OF NEW MEXICO

MAIN FLOOR PLAN

PRISON DIAGRAM

PRELUDE TO A RIOT

December 1979

The show was called Hot Lix and its DJ, Charlie Z, never thought it would be a hit with hardened criminals. All he had in mind was to spin some oldies—the songs he loved growing up while listening to Alan Freed. But over time, organically, the program had been taken over by the inmates at the Penitentiary of New Mexico. They used it as a forum to express their grievances and as a wire service between themselves and the people they loved.

"This next one is from Barbershop, dedicated to his girl in South Valley," Charlie Z would say. "Sandra? Barber's thinking of you tonight."

Buddy Holly and the Crickets: "Words of Love."

Charlie forwarded the messages; he played the requests. During the week his gig was pouring concrete. By the time he arrived at the radio station on Saturdays, his mailbox was teeming with letters. He received over fifty of them per week. Inmates confided in the DJ things they didn't dare tell counseling services inside the pen.

"Yo, Troca, in Cellblock Five. Deborah says she knows you're worried about your appeal. She's been going to Mass every morning, and she's got a good feeling about your new attorney. Keep your chin up, brother."

The Trashmen: "Surfin' Bird."

Radios went for $95 at the prison canteen, an exorbitant price for men making seven cents an hour. Yet everybody had one. They were ubiquitous, both cherished as the sole form of entertainment and despised for the maddening cacophony they created.

"Let's say one guy wants to listen to soul music," an inmate later told the New Mexico State Police, investigating the atmosphere inside the institution in the late 1970s. "Another, Spanish music. Another, rock and roll. Everybody plays their music as loud as they can. You go slowly nuts."

The sound echoed down the central corridor. It reverberated through the minimum- and medium-security dormitories and the maximum-security cellblocks alike. Only on Saturday evenings, when Hot Lix began, did the noise come anywhere close to symphonic. Every dial was tuned to 90.1-KUNM.

"All of the guys . . . consider me a friend," Charlie Z told the newspaper. "And I, in turn, probably know what's going on there more than most people."

It was true. By the late 1970s, Charlie Z knew that the institution had, in very short order, gained a reputation as the worst maximum-security prison in the nation. He knew the PNM, nicknamed "Old Main," sat overcapacity by nearly four hundred men. At the beginning of the 1970s, Cellblock Three, a disciplinary unit, housed thirteen; in only eight years the population had grown to over one hundred: they slept two to three inside seven-by-ten-foot cells. Charlie Z knew that the newcomers, housed in a barracks-style dorm called admissions and orientation (A&O), were so crowded that inmates were forced to sleep on the concrete floors. Fights were common: a hand stepped on, a forehead kicked. He knew the toilets backed up. He knew that small emergency lights meant to illuminate the dorms often shorted out, sending the barracks into total darkness at night. He knew that in that darkness, a pyrexia grew. Scores were settled and drug deals went down. Sexual assaults were rampant.

Because he knew these things, Charlie Z became something of an advocate on behalf of his listeners. By 1979 he intended to host a live show from inside Old Main's fences. "Outta Joint at the Joint," he wanted to call the concert. A Christmas show, Charlie had it slated for Saturday, December 15. He wanted to invite a few cover bands and have inmates live on-air to share their stories. It'd give them a voice. It'd lessen the tension. On December 8, Charlie Z began advertising the concert at the top of every hour.

The concert never took place. On December 9, 1979, while Charlie spun Frankie Avalon and Elvis, the Mills Brothers, and the Ink Spots—while he promoted what he hoped would bring a sense of amity to a penitentiary in dire need of a change—eleven of the most dangerous convicts in the state were using hacksaws to cut through the prison's bars.

■ ■ ■

That December, Montgomery Ward ran an ad in the *Santa Fe New Mexican*: "Hey, Kids! Come Have Breakfast with Santa." The outing was to take place at De Vargas Mall, with breakfast consisting of eggs and toast, a cup of hot chocolate, and a small gift. On the given date, Santa Claus sat on a throne in the middle of the department store while one of his elves staffed chafing dishes. But the breakfast was ill-attended. The eggs went cold. The director of mall operations later said other stores were similarly empty   dead, he called them. When it was suggested to him that perhaps eleven fugitive inmates roaming the streets of town may have been dampening yuletide cheer, the director acquiesced. "It's very sudden and very obvious."

The Lensic Theater downtown suffered troubles of a different kind. The theater was running a new release, *Star Trek: The Motion Picture*, to a crowded audience when, midway through, armed police officers stormed the place. The picture was halted, the houselights turned on. Police went aisle by aisle acting on a tip that one of the absconders was a Trekkie. Nobody of interest was found.

"We offer everything here," the theater manager told the press acerbically, "even forty policemen with shotguns."

Such interruptions had become the norm since December 9, when eleven inmates broke from Old Main. They'd gathered in inmate Jesse Trujillo's cell, located in the so-called maximum-security Cellblock Two. While Trujillo distracted the lone guard on duty within the cellblock, ten other inmates left through pre-sawed bars, made their way onto the roof, and, under the nose of a sleeping guard in the east-facing tower, cut the exterior fence line and let themselves out into the ten miles of plains that separated the institution from the capital city.

Half were convicted murderers, including two inmates, William Jack "Two Pack" Stephens and Michael Colby, who'd recently been convicted of a notorious baseball bat beating inside the penitentiary. Four were in for armed robbery. One was a serial rapist, and one man, Harmon Lee Ellis, was a habitual escapee. All of them were serving sentences that extended beyond natural life expectancy.

The most sought-after gifts that holiday season were the Strawberry Shortcake doll and the Sony Walkman. On TV, Michael Landon shilled for the Kodak Ektralite camera. Car commercials touted miles-per-gallon ratios for perhaps the first time in American history. Around six o'clock on December 12, as Santa Feans left work to find such gifts, cops once again descended. This time it was in the congested area of St. Francis Drive, where a strip mall held a Safeway and a K-Mart. Armed with shotguns, they forced shoppers and employees out into the snow. Chaos ensued; traffic backed up. The police found animatronic Santas, bulbs and balls, canned hams, and eggnog. They found Strawberry Shortcake, but no fugitives.

Police descended. Police converged. Police swarmed.

These were the common lead-ins for evening news and morning papers. More than one hundred law enforcement officers were in town—a task force that included personnel from the penitentiary, city police, the sheriff's office, the National Guard, and additional police from Albuquerque and

Las Vegas—a town just east of Santa Fe. Two National Guard helicopters joined a light airplane in occupying the skies both day and night. The city's notorious roadway infrastructure—not as old as Rome's but just as confusing, with main thoroughfares looping back upon themselves or suddenly ending—hosted frazzling displays of blue lights. Cops rushed from south to north, their cruisers sloshing through ice and snowfall. Police Chief Jesus Sosa asked citizens to check in on their neighbors. He dubbed this call to action Operation Concern. "If you are at work," he said via radio broadcast, "see if that fellow worker is at work [as well] or call on him."

Most people were too afraid to comply. Doors were shut. Lights were turned off. Those with guns stayed up late, drinking coffee and sitting in their living rooms. A woman renting a room on the first floor said she slept with her elderly landlord on the second.

Roadblocks were set up on every major thoroughfare into and out of the city: at the I-25 and the NM-14 interchange, which leads from the prison to the interstate; at I-25 toward Albuquerque; and at I-40 east of Moriarty and down to the south, in Clines Corners. You simply could not leave or enter Santa Fe without being subjected to a thorough search.

"We feel like we're living inside a fortress," a woman told the paper, without irony. The opposite of a fortress is a prison, and that December, the Royal Town of the Holy Faith of Saint Francis of Assisi—known as Santa Fe—was itself a prison.

John Robertson, a staff writer for the *New Mexican*, encapsulated the chaos: "At the peak of rush-hour traffic on St. Michael's, three police cars suddenly pinned in a young man. . . . At gunpoint, the man was forced up against the side of the car and identified. Not one of the hunted, he was abruptly let go."

Somebody reported a man running on the highway shoulder without a shirt on. Police swarmed. He turned out to be a jogger.

"Please suspend jogging until the search is over," Captain Charles Anaya told citizens.

Snowfall gave the city a tiny sense of calm. It was a seasonal commonality: at Christmastime Santa Fe sits beneath low, dark skies, skies that have the effect of muting sound. Winter means snow on the ski lifts, which means happy tourists. It means the burning of farolitos and luminarias: small bonfires made of piñon wood and paper bags filled with sand and candles. They light every part of the city—the walkways and the rooflines of centuries-old adobe structures. The result is a town of white snow and pale adobe and soft incandescence. Santa Fe is a Roman Catholic town, a town as devout to the old religion as any in the nation. The farolitos are a symbolic tradition meant to light the way for Mary and Joseph so that they may find the inn. That the inn would be in this hemisphere and at this elevation is unquestionable to Santa Feans. Their hometown lays claim to the oldest-known statue of the Virgin Mary in the New World.

Weather for the mad weeks before Christmas 1979 was agreeable to the season, if unpredictable. At 8:00 in the morning and then at 3:00 in the afternoon the temperature dropped to zero degrees, with a wind of fourteen miles per hour. By December 13 the temperature hit 50 degrees in the afternoon but quickly dropped below freezing, and a blizzard in Denver came down off the Rockies so that by December 17 the mornings opened in the teens, with heavy snowfall. Fugitives were quickly looking for shelter.

According to Jean Duerlinger writing for the *Santa Fe New Mexican*, around 9:00 on the evening of December 9, less than two hours after the breakout, eighty-one-year-old Richard Dew answered the door to four men, Richard Garcia, Leo McGill, Samuel Mascarenas, and Jesse Trujillo, who asked to use his telephone. They said they needed a tow truck. Before he offered an answer, the men stabbed him twice in the stomach and forced him into his dining room, where they tied him to a chair. They stole a jewelry box, Dew's wallet, a .38 Special, and a shotgun. The four also stole the old man's pickup truck, which had two additional rifles inside the cab. Dew managed to free himself and eventually overcame the stab wounds in the hospital. The inmates made it only halfway to Albuquerque before they were surrounded by police. After a brief standoff, they gave up without firing a shot.

The same afternoon, a woman who kept her horses at Santa Fe Downs went to feed them, only to startle one escapee who was sleeping inside the stable. He beat her and ran away. Police rushed from Richard Dew's house to the racetrack. The criminal justice secretary's office told the press that "every available man" had been sent there; the National Guard scrambled a helicopter, and the task force was accompanied by two citizens, older men who bred and raised bloodhounds. The dogs were given a prison bedsheet to sniff. They soon found the fugitive hiding atop a scrubby, seven-foot mesquite tree, the tree bent over beneath his weight.

By the time of the assault at Santa Fe Downs, seven of the eleven escapees had been captured. Most of the fugitives had been caught within the first few hours, including the notorious pair of Michael Colby and William Jack "Two Pack" Stephens, who'd made it only as far as Cerrillos, twenty miles south of the prison. These recaptures had been relatively peaceful, but the delay in apprehending the remaining four weighed heavily on officials, especially given the final four absconders' backgrounds: Richard Chapman, serving a life term for murder and armed robbery; Harmon Lee Ellis, sixty years for multiple escape attempts; William Norush, five to fifty years as a habitual felon; and William Smith, who had two consecutive life terms for first-degree murder.

By December 13, the mood of Santa Feans quickly turned from fear to fury. Citizens were losing patience with public officials, who appeared to be operating reflexively and lacking any real plan. Governor Bruce King was meant to meet with Democratic presidential candidate Ted Kennedy in Denver, where Kennedy was scheduled to speak to the United Mine Workers of America. But King thought he could save face by remaining in the capital city until the ordeal ended. He'd won the 1978 gubernatorial election by fewer than four thousand votes and had gained a reputation as an addlepated churl: garrulous and charming, but frivolous. Not the man to turn to during a crisis.

By many accounts, King spent his waking hours in front of the television, obsessively watching newsbreaks as well as closed-circuit meetings between legislators and correctional officials. There was a sense that careers, the governor's included, were ending by the hour.

Politicians and administrators turned on each other, deflecting and shifting blame for the escape. In a series of hearings that began on Monday, December 10, and ran through the weekend, Dr. Charles Becknell, criminal justice department secretary, and Deputy Warden Robert Montoya, along with former warden Felix Rodriguez, were brought before various committees to defend themselves. Senator Les Houston opened a hearing of the Legislative Criminal Justice Study Committee by telling Dr. Becknell: "You better clean up that institution immediately, or it's going to be your head on the platter."

Becknell and Rodriguez told the committee that the first step in reform would be a minimum pay raise of $300 a month for each correctional officer. The annual turnover rate for guards at the PNM stood at 80 percent. The COs who remained found themselves outmanned, under-trained, and continually prone to violent attacks—all for an annual salary of $7,000, the lowest in the nation. At county jails and smaller annexes, this number was often as much as $2,000 less. All told, an officer within New Mexico corrections could expect to take home between $583 and $764 per month. This explained the ineptitude that'd led to the breakout, Becknell argued.

The pay issue had been raised before. There had been a number of cases in which the lack of pay was at the root of one of the Corrections Department's other large issues: drug trafficking. One officer, Patrick Vigil, found himself caught within a trafficking ring. His confession to police gave insight into the particulars of the trade. "I received one gold wedding-type band with about six small diamonds, a blue-faced watch. I received two more watches and about one more watch and four rings." In exchange, Vigil sold dimebags to inmates. Other officers told the media you could triple your salary with such arrangements. An inmate estimated that in the year 1975, a kilo of drugs came into the Penitentiary of New Mexico. At the time of the escape, this same inmate said that it had increased to a kilo a month.

There were also allegations that the prison administration was dirty. One such charge was the misappropriation of VA funding for education to inmates enrolled at the College of Santa Fe. One inmate told the newspaper that prisoners were pressured into signing over their benefits to officials; he himself was kept at the prison beyond his release date in order to sign over his VA check. The total amount scraped from the top and disappearing into the coffers of corrections was $25,000 a year.

In an anonymous letter to the *Albuquerque Tribune*, another inmate went into detail about a different scam, this one involving education. The con began with inmates filling out applications for Basic Educational Opportunity Grants (BEOGs), which covered inmates' tuition at a local private school, St. Michael's. But inmates never actually saw the inside of St. Michael's, nor any of the funding. "If you are enrolled and have signed the dotted line, BEOG has sent the check. But a week after enrollment, you get a major report. By policy, you are dropped from the school. Wonderful, more room and money for others. . . ." In other words, the inmate claimed, once the state had sent corrections the grant for your financial aid, you were no longer a source of income; better to select yet another inmate in your place for future enrollment and start the process all over again—eventually writing up this inmate, too, collecting the check, and never having the inmate receive an education.

Representative Colin McMillan responded to Becknell's pay raise argument by calling it unrealistic. Les Houston chastised Becknell for using the prison break as an attempt "to motivate legislation to give you more money." Most bizarre, after these hearings the chairman of the Senate Finance Committee told the press he felt there was a conspiracy afoot: Charles Becknell and the rest of the department had allowed—and even helped mastermind—the escape to strong-arm legislature into granting a new budget.

Unquestionably, these criticisms stemmed from the latent racism of the state. Dr. Becknell was Black, as were several people within his department. In 1979 New Mexico was home to only slightly more than twenty thousand Black people—around 1.5 percent of the state's total population. The senators most vocal in their allegations of advantageous moneygrubbing, laziness, and conspiracy were white and Chicano. As Fred McCaffrey, op-ed writer and reporter on local politics, put it,

> Becknell's job, to put it very bluntly, might be a little easier if his skin was not black, like God made it. That is not to imply that prejudice against Blacks causes all his problems, but it is likely that prejudice against Blacks complicates almost every one of them. When Charles appears before a legislative committee, accompanied by John Ramming, an ex-con, and Michael Banks, another Black, those Legislators of a certain cast of mind, even if they have learned to adopt a veneer of sophistication, must feel a griping in their guts.

Finally, out of frustration, Becknell's closing remarks to the Legislative Finance Committee were that he couldn't "personally sit in front of every institution with a shotgun to prevent escapes."

Despite the terse words and heated arguments, nothing of value came from these hearings.

■ ■ ■

Governor King was not the only one entranced by the political uproar. To the south of the capitol building, on Cordova Road, Harmon Lee Ellis drank cool beer from the refrigerator owned by Betty Toulouse, a woman he'd never met and never would. He hadn't had a beer in seven years. It gave him almost as much satisfaction as the squabbling bureaucrats on TV.

Ellis was forty-four years old, almost twice the age of the other ten inmates who'd escaped from Old Main. He had nothing in common with the rest: they were young, brash, and violent; their records indicated incompatibility with the norms of society. Ellis had once been happily married before his first arrest, in 1958, for robbery. Most likely, Ellis would've been paroled long ago if it weren't for the simple fact that he hated being locked up.

Of course, nobody wants to be in prison. Every inmate responds to such a condition in a unique way. Some calculate good time and early parole and try to cut the time to as short as possible. Others find optimism in the appeals process. More violent inmates, or those given absurdly long terms, decide to adapt to the conditions around them, taking the system for what it is and learning to play the game. Some find religion. Some focus wholly on finding a way to break free.

It is evident in Harmon Lee Ellis's mugshot that he fell into this latter category. All intake photographs show some spectrum of anger, bewilderment, arrogant defiance. Ellis's is different. Looking at his photo, you get a sense of a man who is already contemplating his freedom. It is the image of somebody who is looking beyond you.

He was tall and lean, suffering from male pattern baldness, with a nose flattened by many breaks and home remedied realignments. He needed spectacles to see. Harmon was a Native American from Oklahoma but had been transferred from that state to Arizona and then transferred again on a cooperation agreement to New Mexico. Between 1972 and 1979, he'd tried and failed to escape from various institutions on sixteen separate occasions. His sixteenth attempt had come only ten months earlier, in February. While working in the PNM's furniture plant, Ellis managed to sew himself inside of a sofa. The sofa was transported to New Mexico Highlands University; once there, Ellis cut through the prison van's roof and walked off. He was caught soon after, but by the time he made it to the disciplinary unit at the pen, his fellow convicts had gained an air of respect for his guile.

Old Main lacked gangs, which were becoming popular and problematic in California. But it made up for such with cliques. These cliques were often race-based, often run by native New Mexican Anglos or Chicanos.

Texans did not fit in. Mexican nationals did not fit in. African Americans, comprising a small percentage of the inmate population, were mistrusted and relied on a close-knit circle for defense. Around 1 percent of the population was Indigenous, though the tribal affiliations were nearly wholly Navajo or Hopi. Harmon did not fit in. He was a loner, mostly ignored, until, suddenly, he became a hero. It only made sense for the younger inmates to ask for Ellis's advice. He listened as they laid out their plans, each more convoluted than the last. Stealing CO's uniforms. Having somebody fly a helicopter onto the prison's baseball field. It was likely Ellis who told the rest that sometimes the simplest answer was the best. If they could get out of the cellblock, the fences would be a breeze.

The other inmates didn't believe him at first, but Ellis had done his homework. He knew much of the security at the pen was a facade. He wasn't alone. Later, another inmate discussed the escape with State Police agents: "They started putting out more concertina wire, and a lot of people wondered why. There were less escapes when there wasn't all that wire. I think in a way that's a game people play. They spent all this money . . . we can beat them at it."

The criminals won the game. The younger inmates stole hacksaw blades from an on-site construction renovation, took them to Cellblock Two, and sawed through the bars into the interior crawl spaces, while Hot Lix blared through the corridor. And then, after dinner on December 9, one by one they entered the breached cell and left the institution.

As Ellis had promised, the concertina wire was easy to navigate. Ellis himself had suffered only minor abrasions. Never mind that some of the younger escapees had no plan once free and were apprehended within hours. Ellis's natural loner personality became his best asset. He went from the pen straight to Santa Fe, hung around the southern periphery of the city, and scoped a house where the residents appeared to be gone for the holidays. Once he'd entered the home and read notes scattered around the telephone, he learned his luck was even better. The owner, Betty Toulouse, had been rushed to the hospital and was not expected to return for three weeks. If he were smart, he could wait out the heaviest of the manhunt and perhaps slip away from town once things settled down.

He slept in Toulouse's warm bed. He drank her beer. Under nightfall, he scampered outside to grab the daily newspaper. The paper facetiously asked for clamps on the tongue of the president's rambunctious brother Billy, for the return of the Shah, and for Charles Becknell to realize that the escapees were parolees—"but the paperwork was slow turning up." He watched that week's *Saturday Night Live* featuring Martin Sheen with musical guest David Bowie. The Weekend Update made jokes mostly about gas rationing and the Shah of Iran's gallstones. Ellis finished all of the alcohol in the house that night and fell asleep in a recliner. It was, of his seventeen escapes, the easiest.

■ ■ ■

He likely dreamt of food.

During an investigation months after the breakout, the New Mexico attorney general, Jeff Bingaman, created a task force of police and defense attorneys to interview hundreds of inmates under the assurance of anonymity. At 150 pages, Bingaman's account still serves as a general narrative of the 1980 PNM riot and the precursory issues that led to it. The task force asked for evaluations of nine aspects of life within the prison: canteen, case workers, food services, idleness, the relationship between guards and inmates, medical services, prison industries, psychological services, and recreation. They found deficiencies in every area, but what shocked agents most were the depictions of daily meals.

Most state prisons use kitchen staffing as an enticement for good behavior. The PNM used it either as punitive or entry-level. "You're not supposed to take a mechanic," one inmate told the task force, "and put him in there as a cook if he's never been around a pot in his fucking life." Inmates commonly found cockroaches in their oatmeal and salad. Rocks were in the beans; prisoners chipped teeth. Out at the prison dairy farm, rats drowned in the vats. Jell-O was left out for five or six days, unrefrigerated, and fed to inmates. Even when the inmates were treated to something nice, the pen couldn't get matters right: "One day they were giving out cake and I got me a piece of cake, you know, on my tray. And there was a bunch of little, like, mice footprints all over the frosting, man. And there was rat doo-doo all over it too, man."

In 1976 a Thanksgiving meal led to widespread food poisoning. Inmates described to the attorney general's task force what led to the infamous meal and how the administration chose to handle it:

I pulled some time working in the mess hall and I observed quite a bit of foul treatment of the food. One time in particular I observed a certain staff member pull out a load of turkey that was supposed to be used for Turkey ala King. This turkey looked real bad. It looked green and blue. There was a few of us that were skeptical about eating it but he insisted that the meat was all right, that it'd just been out of the freezer for a little bit. Apparently, the meat was quite bad because I believe half the population attained food poisoning the next morning.

In response, inmates from four of the six dormitories held a peaceful sit-in. The reaction by the administration to the sit-in appeared to be the unintentional encouragement of an inmate uprising. As an inmate told the attorney general's office: "During the food strike, we had some people on the streets [ACLU attorneys] trying to do something and so we were just showing them that we was behind them and we appreciate it and we're trying to help ourselves [by going on strike]. So they [officers] come up there to bust a riot. They said it was a riot. 'Everybody's gonna miss their parole board if they don't go to work, etc.'"

In his book on the riot, *The Devil's Butcher Shop: The New Mexico Prison Uprising*, Roger Morris relays an ominous story told to him by inmates:

At about 5:30 in the evening, the pen is suddenly plunged into darkness while the mess hall is still crowded with prisoners. When the lights come on minutes later, the men, though murmuring and occasionally catcalling, are still sitting or standing passively where the blackout found them. But a special contingent of guards, fully equipped with helmets, shotguns, riot clubs, and tear gas launchers, has quickly materialized in the corridor and at the entrance of the mess. The armed group is made up of what largely inmates call the "goon squad," officers allegedly involved in frequent gang beatings of prisoners. Some of them are not assigned to the . . . shift at that hour, and they have apparently been ready for the blackout. Since nothing develops in the darkness, however, helmeted officers pause awkwardly before the quiet men in the relit hall and then leave as the meal goes on.

After this, the remaining dormitories chose solidarity with fellow convicts, and matters led to a prison-wide hunger strike. "The strike itself was a failure," an inmate told the attorney general's office. "It didn't last very long." This was because the inmates were beaten with axe handles by officers. Even the Protestant chaplain was said to have joined the goon squad. Speaking to the task force, several inmates recalled the ordeal in gruesome detail.

A: The guards that were at the door said, "All of you that don't want in the action, get to the left." Everybody got to the left. "Everybody lie down with your hands [on] your head." They could have come in and there would have been no problem, but then I heard in Spanish they were saying, *ataque*, and I heard *boom-boom*. They shot two canisters. And then *boom boom boom*. I stopped counting at 25. 25. I say, "son-of-a," we thought they were gonna kill us, man. So everybody went to the windows, you know, we're choking, trying to get air and the guards were out there with broomsticks and were hitting us like that so we wouldn't be able to breathe. I thought I was gonna die. Then they come in with the masks and started beating on people with sticks and when you ran out it was like you going to one of those Indian things, you know, you know like on TV—

Q: A gauntlet?

A: Yeah, you know, and they're hitting. I'm lucky because when I ran out I stumbled and I fell and I only got hit on my back. I didn't get hit on the head.

Finally, officers threatened inmates interminably with solitary confinement, or the hole. In New Mexico, the hole consisted of two cells in the basement of Cellblock Three where, rather than bars, the cells had steel doors. The sole, tiny window had a steel latch, which officers could open and close at will. One inmate spoke of how the hole was used after the food strike.

A: I got put in the hole for the [food] strike. They put me in the hole and would feed me one piece of bread or one piece of bologna at five o'clock in the morning and again at five o'clock at night. No mattress or anything. No clothes. Maybe up to six of us inside a cell. We'd have to sleep on each other. All you could use for a pillow would be a person's leg or arm or something.

Q: How long did you stay in?

A: Ten days in the hole.

Q: How many people were inside?

A: The first three days it was two of us, and then, seven days after there were six of us.

Q: And how long did you stay there with five or six guys?

A: About seven days.

Q: Jesus.

A: Mhm.

Q: Everybody just got fed bread and bologna.

A: One piece of bread and one bologna and a cup of milk coffee.

Q: That's a hell of a way to die.

A: I was weighing two hundred pounds, was weightlifting, eating candy and Fritos. And then when I got locked up, I left my muscles down there.

Q: What'd you weigh when you got out of the hole?

A: I was weighing about a hundred and thirty-five pounds.

Q: And you went in at two hundred?

A: Yes, sir. In the ten days I was in the hole, I say I lost about sixty pounds or so.

Harmon had seen these things. He had tried to stay out of them, but he watched. He paid attention. Being an escapee meant knowing the institution you wanted to leave better than anybody—including, or especially, those in charge. And what he was seeing was the crucible of a once-lauded prison, an institution so grand, in fact, the state had called it a point of pride.

There had been a time when, if you were a convicted man, the Penitentiary of New Mexico was the closest you could come to doing easy time. As construction was nearing completion on the facility in 1956, officials were so proud they offered free tours of the facility to anyone who was interested. Warden Harold Swensen implored visitors to bring their sons and daughters. "We're asking parents to bring their children along if the youngsters have reached the age where they can understand the significance of a penitentiary," he said. "The visit may save a child."

And so they came, more than ten thousand citizens, during a sunny weekend in late April. The Madrid Highway was choked with pickups and station wagons—whole nuclear families curious to see the new prison. Once behind the perimeter fencing, they played with the grilles and sat on convict cots. Some tourists accidentally locked themselves inside sensory deprivation units. One teenage girl said she liked the place but thought the cells were too small. Paul Madigan, acting warden of Alcatraz, flew to Santa Fe to offer his blessing. The governor gave a short speech. The *Roswell Record* called the spectacle a "weird scene." Throngs waited to have their picture taken inside the gas chamber. A confused young boy sat on the death chair and shouted, "Look, Grandma! I'm being *electrocuted!*"

Interim Deputy Warden W. M. Brown, a PhD in clinical psychology from the University of Oregon, told the press the new prison would allow inmates to receive their high school diplomas and gain college degrees, and would use the Dale Carnegie course to aid inmates in returning to civilization. "It is the responsibility of society to keep a man, if he is convicted of violating the law, locked up for a period of time. In addition, there is also the responsibility to return him to society so that he may be a responsible citizen."

Warden Brown went on to say that no penal institution on the planet had a more advanced approach to rehabilitation than that in New Mexico. Throughout the 1950s and '60s, the Penitentiary of New Mexico functioned as a leading example of rehabilitative and progressive reform. Prisoners suffering from mental illness thrived under Project Newgate, something Brown had helped develop while working in corrections in Oregon and implemented in New Mexico. The program offered a systemic counseling program as well as tutoring and ACT test preparation for those interested in college. There were opportunities for skilled labor as well. As sociologist Mark Colvin wrote, "Training in auto body repair, carpentry, mechanics, plumbing, welding, and electronics were provided. In September 1969, a computer keypunching operation was opened." The program, developed by IBM, taught inmates data entry. Soon these inmates were doing all the work for the state's data processing center. Those with drug and alcohol addictions were also flourishing. AA meetings met regularly and the organization held an annual banquet: wives, children, and close friends were allowed to attend, with the kitchen staff offering a generous dinner menu. A group of former disciplinary problem inmates were put on the masthead of *Enchanted News*, the prison's monthly newspaper. Quickly, their attention moved away from fighting and drugs, as they were given nearly free rein to investigate even staff members.

These initiatives had an enormous impact on recidivism. According to the US Department of Justice's Bureau of Justice Statistics, the number of people incarcerated in New Mexico in 1960 stood at 1,260. By 1970, this number had fallen by nearly one-third, and all projections had this decrease continuing into the future. Men housed at Old Main simultaneously served their debt to society while learning skills that, once paroled, made them an asset in the workforce. Through psychological services, religious programs, and substance abuse therapy, they moved beyond the troubles that had brought them into the system.

A good job, an education. There was a baseball diamond and a mini-golf course.

And food. Fresh food. For breakfast, inmates were offered coffee, fresh milk, applesauce, fried eggs, hash browns, and biscuits. For lunch: pot roast with brown gravy, mashed potatoes, creamed corn, a beet and onion salad, bread, and chocolate ice cream. At suppertime the cafeteria would have fresh fish and tartar sauce, Lyonnaise potatoes, lima beans, cabbage salad, bread, and, for dessert, coconut squares. The menu changed every day. The cafeteria was supplied by the Farm, a working finca in Las Lunas manned by well-behaved inmates. New Mexico is a ranching and farming state, and those inmates who had no prior convictions nor escape elements could pursue the very real occupation of agriculture while locked up. Here, cowboys and vaqueros broke horses and rode herd over cattle; they raised multiple crops—all without guards or bars or fences. The Farm produced 97,000 gallons of milk and 32,000 pounds of beef per year. It produced 42,000 pounds of pork and 20,000 pounds of pinto beans; there were enormous supplies of green chiles, cucumbers, garlic, lettuce, green onions, bell peppers, radishes, and watermelons—much of this bounty to be delivered back to the prison kitchen.

Warden Harold A. Cox was so proud of his institution, he gave the *Carlsbad Current-Argus* a grandiose statement: the men inside his walls were better off than they would have been as freemen. His prison gave them the "most healthful" life they could imagine:

Men keep regular hours, indulge in no alcoholic beverages, take no harmful drugs, eat nutritious food served at regular intervals, keep busy at assigned tasks, receive immediate medical attention when they are ill, take plenty of exercise, and are given the opportunity for adequate rest in comfortable beds inside buildings that are warm in winter and cool in summer and so well-ventilated that the air is changed every 30 seconds. They are exposed to no infections as they would be in a free society. . . . They can discuss spiritual problems with a priest or minister, and they can discuss emotional and personal problems with trained counselors. So they are beset by far fewer stressors than they were before they were sentenced.

So what happened? Where had that all been since Harmon Ellis arrived at Old Main? When had the beans turned to rocks, and the milk to drowned rats?

The years 1972–73 are often marked by criminologists as a watershed in American penal practice. A report conducted by the PEW Center on the States on recidivism begins: "Since the early 1970s, prisons have been the weapon of choice in America's fight against crime." The report goes on to pinpoint 1973 as the year everything changed. Departing from President Lyndon B. Johnson's focus on poverty as the root cause of criminality, then president Richard Nixon took a hard-line stance against criminal acts themselves, especially drug possession and distribution. He created the Drug Enforcement Agency (DEA) in July 1973. Policymakers on both sides fell in lockstep, advocating for and winning elections by supporting harsh penalties for possession. The nation witnessed the "tough on crime" mantra and supported it. Since the creation of the DEA, the nation's incarceration numbers have grown by 705 percent.

By the time of the December 1979 escape, the PNM, built to house 800 inmates, housed 1,150. If that wasn't enough, the mid-seventies oil crises began the worst recession in a half century. New Mexico's unemployment in that sector rose 87 percent over the previous three decades. While the state's Department of Workforce Solutions received high numbers of unemployment assistance, poverty initiatives were abandoned by legislators. So, too, were funds for corrections. While prisons filled, the budgets to run them disappeared. Old Main was not spared. Incentive programs like Newgate and College Release were cut. The data processing program was cut. Three-quarters of the inmate population went idle, not even offered jobs in the machine plant. The cuts infiltrated the administration. Between 1970 and 1980, seven separate men served as New Mexico's Executive of Corrections. As one inmate later told the attorney general's office, "It was too big of a transition [from one administration to the next]. Too big of a change, too radical of a change." These radical transitions from ethos to ethos led to bitterness within the inmate population. Or perhaps it was rage. Whatever the feeling at Old Main that December, Ellis knew he wanted to be far away from it.

■ ■ ■

Around lunchtime on December 20, eleven days after the breakout, Harmon Ellis was awakened by knocking on the front door of Betty Toulouse's house. It was George and Alice Milner, the next-door neighbors. They were acting on Operation Concern.

Ellis had on him a kitchen knife, but no time to find cover. He'd made it behind the sofa when the front door opened. Alice and George soon found him. In the ensuing tussle, Harmon Ellis cut Alice with the kitchen knife—later claiming it was an accident. After that, the Milners acquiesced. Ellis had them sit on the floor.

"You've just caused me a problem," he told them.

The Milners begged not to be hurt. Ellis told them he wasn't a violent man. They asked that, if he were to take them hostage, to do so in their own home. Ellis thought it over, and then yielded. He marched them next door. There, he tied Alice to George with pantyhose, because Alice complained of poor circulation and the damage duct tape might cause. For the next two days they watched television. Harmon ate voraciously.

On December 22, for reasons that remain unclear, Ellis finally sighed and stood and took $100 from George Milner's wallet and the keys to the couple's Cadillac. He left the house on Cordova Road without a word. He traveled west and then south, taking Highway 285 out of town. The route swiftly drops down out of the Sangre de Cristo Mountains and into a vast gorge freckled every so often with sharp, pink cliffsides that dazzle and change hue as the sun moves across the high desert sky. Every few miles traffic signs warn of falling boulders. The wind is tremendous here and comes down from both the Rockies and El Cerro de la Coseña.

Any semblance of Santa Fe disappeared. Ellis relaxed. Down here there was nothing but centuries-old rancheros and antelope. The radio did not play Hot Lix. Instead, it spoke of the Ayatollah and the oil crisis.

One can only speculate as to Harmon Ellis's plan. He never spoke about it to investigators or journalists. He never revealed where he was going or why. What is known is that his freedom ended where Highway 285 intersects with Route 66. There, a man named Roy Cline established an enormous gas station / restaurant / knickknack store. It was there, too, that Santa Fe's finest had set up a roadblock.

Ellis surrendered peacefully. In the photo that appeared in the *Albuquerque Journal*, he is wearing a heavy coat, and what's left of his hair is ruffled from both the wind and the police. He has on his spectacles. When a journalist asked if he had any regrets, he said only that he wished he hadn't been caught.

He was the eighth of the eleven fugitives to be captured. It would be another three weeks before Richard Chapman and William Norush were apprehended in Blackfoot, Idaho, in a motel room overlooking the Snake River. And it would take five months for the final escapee, murderer William Smith, to be apprehended at a bar in Waikiki, Hawaii (an undercover police officer overheard Smith, then going by the name Richard Cutler, trying to buy a handgun and solicit murder-for-hire contracts). But it was the capture of Harmon Ellis that led to a communal catharsis. He was labeled as the mastermind, the poster child of the escape. The Duke of Disappearances, an op-ed writer called him. The Houdini of Hacksaws. "Every morning, I expect to have a cup of coffee with him at the doughnut shop," the writer concluded.

Upon his arrest in Clines Corners, politicians felt both congratulative of each other and reassuring to the population. In the weeks that followed, Bruce King sponsored and passed a bill that pumped millions of dollars into renovation projects at Old Main. They would begin by renovating the cellblocks, where hardened inmates were housed apart from medium-security inmates, who lived in dormitories. Representatives told Santa Feans and, for that matter, the rest of the state that the public would never have to worry about what was happening at the penitentiary. This had all been a frightening but momentary blip. In that respect, they were lucky, King said.

In thinking of Harmon Ellis's decision to head toward Cline's Corners, it becomes impossible to overlook the eventuality of his capture. He must have known the roadblock would be there. He had to have known it. Shortly after his detention, Harmon Lee Ellis was transferred back to Arizona. He died there in 1992 of natural causes, having never attempted an escape again. The escape failed, but the attempt made Harmon Ellis one of the luckiest men in the system. By 1980, he was no longer on the roster as a prisoner at the Penitentiary of New Mexico.

In Santa Fe, the escape was soon forgotten. The pews that year were filled for Christmas Mass.

PART ONE

CHAPTER ONE

The highway just north of Carlsbad, New Mexico, a stretch of US Route 285, is known as the Seven Rivers Highway, though there are not and never have been seven rivers here. There once was an inchoate town named as much, a place where John Chisum and other legendary cattlemen let their herds cool in the shade of the pecan trees. Later, Seven Rivers served as a refuge for outlaws during the Lincoln County War. But the town is gone. A dam was built, and the old location now lies thirty feet below a reservoir. Carlsbad itself sits on the dusty plains east of the Guadalupe Escarpment, where the mountain range fizzles to a yield of stubby little mesas. It is a lonesome and arid place, making up for what it lacks in verdant beauty by way of dust storms and scorpion hordes. It is home to both my maternal and paternal families. They settled here for the cattle and mining industries, but it is difficult to look out upon the biome and fathom why anybody, even the most desperate of souls, would choose this spot to put down stakes.

This is not God's country. Today, local headlines declare: "Lethal Rattlesnakes on the Rise." And posters stapled downtown from the Crime Stoppers of Eddy County alert the public to a spate of cattle killings. The livestock were shot for jollies and left in the sun to bloat. "Upon arrival, law enforcement found six head killed." The poster claims, "Each cow worth $17,000 to $20,000 dollars [sic]." Historically, the local economy depended on such livestock as well as hay and pecans. In the late 1970s and early 1980s, Eddy County became home to the Waste Isolation Pilot Plant (WIPP), the country's only "deep geological repository for transuranic radioactive waste." It is an underground landfill for the Department of Energy, a place to bury sundries contaminated with plutonium. In an essay on the plant, Edward McPherson writes that " . . . when it is completed and sealed, WIPP will become a monument to man-made poison, a time capsule of our own folly." It was my grandfather, Louis Whitlock, a state senator, who headed the legislation that landed Carlsbad this monument of folly.

WIPP is still a popular economic piston, but the most recent thrust—the one that, today, has made Carlsbad a boomtown—is hydraulic fracturing. While the use of high-powered brine to destroy rock has created a seemingly unending profit for natural gas concerns, the process does not come without consequences: a sinkhole has opened on the south side of town. Though relatively small now, geologists have reported to the *Los Angeles Times* that "at any moment . . . the cavity could collapse . . . taking with it a chunk of highway, a church, several businesses, and the El Dorado Estates trailer park."

If none of this is visceral enough, I'll add a personal anecdote: a few years ago, my father and I were traveling through Eddy County when a flash thunderstorm began. The storm lulled me to sleep; soon, my father nudged me. "Look out there." The highway in front of us was alive with dark rondures, each the size of a billiards ball. "Tarantulas," he told me. There were thousands of them, a nation, scurrying from the shoulder of the highway across the pavement in front of our roaring Dodge Ram. In the autumn this area of the northern Chihuahuan Desert is a prime breeding location for the arachnids. On this day the cool air had lured them from their dens and tricked them of the season. You could not see beyond them, but I happened to glance in the passenger side mirror the path we were cutting through their ranks.

It is a country, then, of freaky invertebrates and nuclear fallout and violence to quell boredom. And beneath it all the ground itself, once viewed by cattlemen as hardened and irresolute, is now threatening to crumble.

Highway 285 offers the only northbound route out of Carlsbad. It is a straight 270-mile shot to the capital city and cultural hub of Santa Fe. But a seventy-mile stretch between Roswell and Vaughn is as notorious to New Mexicans as the Khumbu Icefall is to alpinists. There are no towns or gas stations, no landmarks by which to judge your location. There are no emergency services and no cellular coverage. The Sierra Blanca and Sacramento mountain ranges come together eighty miles west. Across the flat terrain the ranges are the color of a deep bruise, almost touchable but not. They remain distant, a tease of beauty in an otherwise ugly landscape; until, of course, massive supercells barrel down from the range's altitude and race toward you, picking up speed and blocking out the sun.

On the first day of 1985, rancher Charles Martin woke with a feeling that his herd was in trouble. The day before, Martin had listened to the radio as meteorologists warned those in Chaves County that the year would end with a blizzard, and indeed, late in the afternoon the bank marquee in downtown Roswell read 6 degrees. By sundown, the winds were tremendous, and a gnarly snowstorm engulfed Poverty Flats, Charles Martin's cattle ranch. As he'd expected, a group of mostly calves had gotten spooked by the storm and had wandered far from the dry barn down to an arroyo where they often huddled when scared. After breakfast, Martin drove his pickup to the arroyo. "That's when I first saw them boots," he told me. "They was a fancy pair, ostrich maybe, with gold tips on them."

That morning was still brutally cold, but the wind had died down and the sun was out, glinting off snow mounds and the Spanish-style toe rands of these boots. As Martin approached, he realized they weren't empty.

"I used the CB from my truck to call the sheriff. I told him he didn't need to bring an ambulance or anything. All he'd need to bring with him was a rake and a trash sack. That's how much of the fella was left. Well, lo and behold, the sheriff comes out here with a posse. Seven carloads of boys."

The scene left Charles Martin stupefied. People disappeared out here. It was rare and unfortunate, but it happened. This was especially true for migrant workers, whom Martin both employed and had seen traversing his land on the way to a lucrative job that more often than not proved a fool's errand. The number of officials seemed to him an overexertion. He wasn't happy to find that he was pushed out of the narrative: he was offered no information about exactly who or what he'd stumbled across.

The remains were transferred back to Roswell. There, the coroner listed the man's personal items: a velour shirt and blue jeans, a turquoise pinky ring, and the shell of a 30.06 with the bolt untethered and, in its place, a cocaine spoon. There were also the boots, size 10.5, but hardly more than a skeletonized body. Nevertheless, the coroner ascertained that the man's knees had both been intentionally shattered. It was likely that the body had been dumped on Charles Martin's property. He was not a lonesome and unlucky drifter passing through the badlands on his way to California. Nor was he a stranger to police or to the state of New Mexico. The decedent, identified through dental records, was a twenty-six-year-old from Carlsbad named Gary Dru Williams, a man who'd gone missing half a decade earlier.

It is highly likely that the sheriff's posse called by Charles Martin was less than enthused to have this particular body on their hands. It meant investigating his death. And investigating the death of Gary Dru Williams meant reopening a wound that hadn't yet had an opportunity to become a scar—a less-than-half-a-decade-old abrasion still pustulating, known as the Riot at Old Main. The state was still reeling from the nightmare. And the state wanted nothing more than for the populace to forget the ordeal and the men who'd suffered from the undesirable distinction of having been witness to the nation's most violent prison riot. Men like Gary Dru Williams.

CHAPTER TWO

Just before 6:00 on a Friday morning four years earlier, in 1980, Gary Williams had ridden past Charles Martin's ranch as a passenger inside a dilapidated van owned by the Corrections Department. He wore blue coveralls marked NMCD. His ankles were shackled, and a leather belt fitted with a D ring, secured around his waist and from his ankles to his handcuffs, locked his wrists to the belt. His next stop would be the admissions and orientation unit on the south wing of the Penitentiary of New Mexico in Santa Fe.

It was all a bit melodramatic. The inmate in custody was overweight, prematurely balding, a loner without much drive. Gary Williams had never been in trouble with the law before. He was nonviolent and unlikely to commit any future crimes.

Williams had been found guilty of attempted arson one week before, on January 26, 1980. On the advice of Gary's father, A. W. "Dubb" Williams, a businessman who believed the arson scheme would lead to easy money, Gary had agreed to help burn down a family friend's business, Roger Jenkins's Steam Laundry. The three men would then split the earnings from the subsequent insurance payout—estimated at $75,000 per man in today's terms.

Gary had always slipped through life without notice. It was as though his presence unnerved the people who actually took the time to consider him. Thus, his father had assumed Gary to be an excellent accomplice to the crime.

None of this would have weighed on Gary except for his familial circumstances. He was born August 24, 1952, to A. W. "Dubb" Williams and his wife, LaDon Garrett. The family added another son, Jeffrey Lloyd, in 1956. In nearly every conceivable way, it was an idyllic childhood, with a father who seemed to make the newspaper fairly often. LaDon and Dubb, and by extension the entire Williams family, were prominent and socialized with other prominent people, such as Roger and Ginger Jenkins.

In those early years, sometime between the 1950s and the late 1960s, there is a photograph of Dubb and Roger Jenkins. The occasion is the visit of five mayors from Iran touring the American interior. Days before, the traveling group had inspected flour mills and meat packing plants in Augusta, Kansas, before moving on to Billings, where they were offered an extensive tour of the landfill. Now they were in Carlsbad. The contingent had come to an arid town with interest in the irrigation system. For the arriving mayors, their care fell to the hands of a group called the Goldcoaters, a platoon of prolix yokels affiliated with the Chamber of Commerce.

Dubb and Roger were granted the honor of hosting. Choosing Roger Jenkins to host was a no-brainer: the Eddy County sheriff's posse had bestowed upon him the high honor of chairman of the Barbecue Salad Committee.

Both had grown up exceedingly poor—Roger in the tiny Mississippi Delta town of Ripley, Tennessee; Dubb in Blanco, Oklahoma, a town of fewer than one hundred citizens situated in the foothills and hollows of the Ouachita Mountains in Arkansas. Jenkins was born in 1920, Dubb seven years later. This meant they both spent their childhood in the Deep South Depression and the Dust Bowl. To escape their circumstances, both men volunteered for military service and entered World War II.

Once the war ended, Roger moved to Texas and married a local gal named Ginger. Soon the couple moved west and opened Carlsbad Steam Laundry at 408 S. Canal Street—Canal being the main road in town. Ginger ran the books. Roger shook hands. The tough work inside the laundry was doled out to poor Hispanics who lived south of town in an area known as San Jose, the name deriving from the local Catholic Church, a scant three miles but worlds away from Roger and Ginger's home on Riverside.

For the Jenkins's, the money came fast and free-flowing. It felt almost sinful. Perhaps as atonement, both became civic-minded.

Ginger was an active member in the Daughters of the Nile, Alpha Mu, Beta Sigma Fi, and the Hospital Auxiliary. Roger donated a cake for the Memorial Hospital's sixty-third anniversary celebration. He was elected vice chair of a committee to promote the Carlsbad Convention Center to a national audience. At the Juarez Country Club, just over the border in Mexico, he was named president of the US Highway 180 Association. The association, known soon thereafter as Amigos Across the Border, was a group of politicians and businesspeople from both Mexico and the American Southwest who wanted to boost "friendships, business, and other areas than tourism."

As for Dubb, after the war he matriculated into Eastern New Mexico State College on the G.I. Bill. There, he met LaDon Garrett, the daughter of a well-to-do lumberman from Carlsbad. They married and moved to her hometown, where Dubb worked for his father-in-law. Wanting to become his own man, he saved money to open a Gibson's department store, half a mile south of Jenkins's laundry. Like Roger, Dubb flourished. It took no time at all for them to run in the same circle.

And, like Roger, Dubb was civic-minded. When one of the Rotary Club's Wild Cow Milking Contest team members—a group that, for charity, was taxed with catching a wild cow and milking it—had to travel for business, Dubb Williams stepped into their place. In pictures, Dubb and LaDon stand looking proud of this accomplishment. And in other pictures, ones that pitted the Rotary Club against the Kiwanis in a softball game, Dubb looks even happier to be given coaching on balls and strikes from a woman to whom he was not married.

Ginger and LaDon grew close as well. LaDon was named president of the Xi Tau chapter of Beta Sigma Phi. She regularly hosted a women's club in her home. The one-act play "The Lost Silk Hat" was performed in her living room to the delight of the club.

Roger loomed tall and gentle. Dubb was short and a bit hard, with firm, calloused hands. He liked to work on cars. He was sometimes keen to wear denim overalls with penny loafers and white athletic socks. Nonetheless, they were drawn to each other for their hardscrabble backgrounds. This was often the case in the southern region of the state. There is no old money in New Mexico—at least not in the badlands. The men who would eventually run Carlsbad, replacing each other as mayors or as chairmen on this and that committee, had all reached a dream beyond their dreams. Yes, the location was odd. They might've envisioned penthouses in Manhattan, or a getaway villa in Palm Springs, or both. But what did it matter? The accoutrements were the same. Despite the stink at night of burning creosote or tar residue when the wind blew a certain way, this group of men had found their place.

No, it was more than that.

There must have been something divine involved.

This ugly, useless place changed in 1925 when geologists looking for oil found instead an abundance of sulfur and potash deposits deep beneath the desert floor. (Pronounced *pot-ash*, for that which it succeeded, the mineral is widely used in industrial fertilizers.) Now known as the Delaware Basin, this area was once a prehistoric ocean floor where all manner of strange creatures decayed. Nine years after its discovery, the Department of the Interior labeled this the Potash Area and gave managerial rights to the Bureau of Land Management. By the end of World War II, Eddy County's only competition in the potash industry was the entire nation of Canada.

And while a shepherd named Jim White had stumbled upon a massive cave system south of town in 1898, the discovery remained something of an anomaly for decades. It was not until 1925, the same year of the potash discovery, that President Calvin Coolidge created the Carlsbad Cave National Monument. Later, with the expansion of the American interstate highway system, Carlsbad became a top destination on the great American family road trip. A history of the National Parks Service describes the importance of the caverns to the national ethos of the time:

> Carlsbad Caverns represented the attainment of American ideals. Its role as geologic curiosity expanded into a designation as a mid-century wonder. In 1903, Theodore Roosevelt said of the Grand Canyon: "It is a place that every American, if he can travel, should see." By the 1970s, Carlsbad Caverns had joined that category for the broader, automobile-based traveling public. It had become an indicator of belonging to the expanding middle class, a site that Americans had to see if only to think of themselves as enjoying the fruits of post-war society's opulence.

By 1961, the caverns had welcomed its ten millionth visitor while the mines had welcomed a throng of eager young physicists and geologists, engineers of all stripes—many of them able to pursue advanced degrees thanks to the G.I. Bill. They brought with them not only a desire for shopping and dining and cinema but for *good* shopping and *fine* dining and *complex* cinema.

Between this strong, emerging upper-middle class and the tourist industry, it took no time at all for locals like Dubb to figure out you did not need a master's degree in geology to be successful. Entrepreneurs preyed upon the lore so many traveled thousands of miles to experience. Cactus Bowling Lanes, with its enormous saguaro sign blitzing the night (never mind that saguaro are not found in New Mexico). The Arrowhead Drive-In. The Totem Hut. The

Apache Trading Post, with moccasins in sizes for the whole family. Blount's Restaurant, serving up "chicken steaks." The Motel Stevens boasted of seven acres of rooms and suites, playgrounds, cocktail lounges, swimming pools, and five-channel television. The night skies of Carlsbad were ink-smeared with bats zigzagging for insects attracted to the neon glare of motor inns and bars. There were psychics, curanderos, arrowhead archaeology tours, rattlesnake pits, and a town called White's City that sat at the base of the national park. Anybody who visited Carlsbad Caverns had to pass through White's City; many chose to rent one of the adobe bungalows cut into the lechuguilla-dense mesas. Despite having its own postal code, White's City was not a city. It was a classic tourist trap, a place to buy T-shirts and hats fashioned with bat wings or to browse the Million Dollar Museum, where one could view old farm equipment and a hallway of taxidermy, test their skills on the Kiss-O-Meter (for a dime the player would squeeze a handle that measured your smooching ability—anywhere from Hot Stuff to Sloppy Sour), and gawk at the pièce de résistance: a jarred fetus once proclaimed to be, among other things, an alien baby. "No one is sure exactly when the museum acquired this artifact," its label read, "but it does not appear to be human."

There was a sense, then, that Carlsbad had been anointed by the natural world, that it was not to suffer the fates of its sister cities such as Artesia and Hobbs and Loving, which, lacking such a blessed underworld, were forever dependent on the boom-and-bust of beef prices and commodities futures. Here you needed only a modicum of ingenuity and the Good Lord on High would shed his prosperity upon thee.

Such was the milieu I see when I look at the photograph of Roger and Dubb and their guests from Iran: Roger and Dubb have ignored a luncheon, opting instead to escort these five mayors, each dressed in immaculate French-designed black suits and French-designed black ties, down the long sloping St. Augustine of Roger's backyard to his boat slip on the Pecos River. Roger, stripped of his gold blazer, wearing a short-sleeved dress shirt and a pair of Wayfarers, grins proudly from behind the steering wheel of his speedboat. The mayors are with him; their stern faces are now filled with exhilaration as they wave to the photographer. The interpreter, a graduate student from Columbia sitting next to Roger, looks either frightened or nauseated. But Roger has the face of a man in charge.

These were the progenitors, the men Gary, firstborn, was meant to emulate.

■■■

Whatever blessings the Carlsbad entrepreneurial class may have felt were gone by the late 1970s. The president had appeared on television in a cardigan, asking the American people to conserve energy. For a region dependent on energy consumption, the 1973 and, later, 1979 crises hit hard.

By 1978, Roger Jenkins's Steam Laundry was facing bankruptcy. He spent that year in duress. Jenkins had done a marvelous job of ridding himself of the poverty he'd faced in childhood: he now owned one of the premiere homes in town and drove a black Cadillac he kept immaculately clean. His beauty of a wife, Ginger, was rarely without her beloved gray poodle. When his friends began buying Cessna airplanes, Jenkins bought a bigger one (he had no formal training as a pilot and sold the plane after nearly wrecking it in the Guadalupe Mountains). Now all of it was in jeopardy. Jenkins had no interest in returning to his former life. And so, on an afternoon in January 1979, Roger Jenkins pulled his Cadillac behind Dubb's department store and told Dubb he was serious about the Steam Laundry. He wanted to burn it down.

Dubb was loyal to a fault. Roger did not have to ask twice. Besides, the two men were buddies with every attorney in town and campaign donors for the sheriff's reelection bid. They saw themselves as untouchable. Further, their closest buddies had had insurance companies pay out. In a few short years, the Arrowhead Drive-In burned down. Later, Marchione's Italian Restaurant burned down. Cactus Lanes partially burned. Zaffer's burned. The Deluxe Café burned. So few of these incidences had been successfully prosecuted that in private, people began referring to arson as the Carlsbad Retirement Plan.

Winters in southern New Mexico tend not to bring crispness to the air or a desire for cable-knits. Rather, the dried arroyos flood. Cattle drown. Half-ton pickups wash away, never to be seen again. Or the summer swelter lasts beyond Christmas. The second week of January 1979 began with temperatures near freezing. Roger and Dubb and Gary met each night in Gary's tiny trailer, crowding around the space heater and working out their plan.

Roger and Dubb had been so certain. The plans were simple. Roger would drive his Cadillac back to Ripley and call Carlsbad police lieutenant Bill Sadler, a friend, under unrelated auspices. Dubb had taken a box of hair dye from his own store and turned his blond-gone-white locks jet black. Soon he'd drive down to El Paso, to Yearwood Auto Supply, where he'd purchase gallons of Moroso Octane Booster—a highly flammable additive for racecar engines. (Though he did his best to remain nonchalant, the salesman later told investigators "the man offered, in effect, a confused and improbable account of the purpose to which he intended to put the octane booster," adding that the quantity was "very unusual." When offered a photograph of A. W. Williams, the associate said: "This face looks familiar, this looks like him, but the hair is grayer.") He'd then place the octane booster in the back room of the laundry, and on the night of January 12, 1979, Gary would find the back door unlocked, pour the booster into a trombone sprayer, and, by lighting a stack of invoices, let chemistry take over.

January 12 must've passed slowly for Gary. He lay in his bed, staring at the ceiling of his trailer. He filled the ashtray. He was not his brother. Gary lacked a constitution for criminality. It was possible he would have backed out of the plan, but for the first time in his life his father was counting on him. Aside from his cut in the insurance gain (roughly $75,000 when adjusted for inflation), the promise was to be made in a Carlsbad sort of way. To be on the inside with the men who ran town. If he could not make it in Toledo, perhaps he could make it back here. He allowed that the prospect outweighed his fear. After all, he was surrounded by men who took risks and skirted laws, and from all indications, they'd been rewarded.

That night Gary put on a coat and a pair of tennis shoes and drove north and parked behind the Steam Laundry. Roger Jenkins had snipped the wires to the laundry's neon sign and interior lights. Jenkins had also turned off the alarm system. Gary had a key to the back door. Beneath a tarp and some mopheads he found the Moroso Octane Booster, five gallons of paint thinner, and the sprayer.

Alone and in the dark, Gary sprayed the booster in the back room. He worked his way through the building. When he came to Roger's office, which was locked, he climbed up onto shelves and forced himself through the threshold of a broken transom window. This was Roger's idea. He was not so naive as to think the fire would be categorized as an accident, but he wanted the police to believe the arsonist was somebody young and agile, a disgruntled worker, perhaps, or maybe just a local speed freak. The problem was that while Gary was young, he could not under any terms have been described as agile. He had your standard fat man's loafing gait to him, and when he had to run, which was never, it was in a pained fashion, a kind of rolling from one fallen arch to another. It comes as no surprise, then, that, in his attempt to breach the broken transom window, Gary lost his balance and hit the floor of the office. The trombone sprayer came down with him, exploding, sending the accelerant everywhere. His clothes and shoes were soaked.

He composed himself. He sprayed Jenkins's office, including some dress shirts Roger kept on a rack. Once done, he left the containers and headed back to the rear entrance, tracking the soles of his sneakers throughout the premises. In the back room, scared, and finally understanding what he was doing, Gary lit the invoices and fled. Back at his trailer, he tried to drink himself calm and watched the sun rise.

"If you don't know anything about cars," Attorney Dick Blenden told me, "then you wouldn't know what the hell Moroso Octane Booster is, because I didn't, either." Blenden, who opened a criminal defense practice in Carlsbad in 1962, was hired by Roger Jenkins two days after the failed arson attempt. As Blenden explained to me, "You pour it in an automobile and it ignites when it's four hundred degrees. So some Phi Beta Kappa goes in and gets it and thinks they're going to scatter it around [Jenkins's store] and it's going to accelerate the fire. Well, horseshit." According to Blenden, the booster never ignited. Later testimony from the state described the total damage: "Only one cabinet had been scorched and some papers had been burned."

This was the totality of the scheme's effectiveness. When Jenkins was called by police and told of the arson attempt, Blenden stated, "Roger's immediate reaction was 'Well, I didn't have anything to do with it!'" Blenden laughed. He said, "Really, a brilliant comment."

Roger had hired Dick Blenden; Dubb turned, as he often did, to a defense attorney named Tom Cherryhomes. Dick Blenden and Tom Cherryhomes were the Dream Team for the Fifth Judicial District Court of New Mexico. Blenden wore a chestnut toupee and big false teeth. Born in a terrible and tiny town in West Texas, he was intelligent but displayed the kind of country witticisms that appealed to any roughneck or cowboy sitting on a jury panel. He knew exactly at what plane one can talk above somebody without being perceived as haughty. Dick Blenden's notoriety as a drinker paled only to his reputation inside courtrooms. He was perhaps the most renowned criminal defense attorney in the Desert Southwest. He was a master at the bon mot and thus fantastic at giving wedding toasts—even better at eulogies. He was charming, in other words, a kind of cirrhotic

Matlock. The drinking may have been an asset: Dick Blenden spent so many hours in bars he recognized the kinds of secrets people revealed after three doubles and the inspiration of a sad country-Western ballad. Tom Cherryhomes was a force of nature. Ned Cantwell, the former publisher of the *Current-Argus*, described the attorney to me thusly: "Tom was a pretty good buddy. Boyish, charming, Hollywood pretty, a tall guy with an athletic body, strong as an ox. All that strength linked to an incendiary temper was his undoing. He once grabbed an opposing attorney and pinned him, legs dangling, against the courtroom wall."

Cantwell meant this in a literal sense. In 1985 the New Mexico Supreme Court wrote a formal reprimand against Cherryhomes, citing "three separate incidences where you failed to control your temper and where you verbally and physically abused persons who were participants in legal proceedings in which you were involved." The third incident nearly led to Cherryhomes physically assaulting Judge William Fort during a cross-examination.

> COURT: And the jury, what, what the court is trying to tell you [Cherryhomes], if you will just keep quiet long enough for me to make a record, is that there's nothing in the file in the jury verdict that says on what basis they found. They may have found—
>
> CHERRYHOMES: Who cares, Judge?
>
> COURT: All right, just a moment, counselor, and I'm going to order you not to say anything when I talk. You are disrupting the orderly pro—get back to where you were and do not approach the bench. I am ordering you to go back to that witness stand, I mean to go back to that rostrum and do not approach the bench. Do you hear me, counselor? Let the record show that counselor is not moving.
>
> CHERRYHOMES: Oh, I'm moving.
>
> COURT: Let the record show that counselor is moving very slow.
>
> CHERRYHOMES: I'm just not moving very fast. How fast would you like me to move, Judge? Would you like me to jump?
>
> COURT: Counselor—
>
> CHERRYHOMES: I might fall.
>
> COURT: Counselor—
>
> CHERRYHOMES: One of these days, Judge, you're going to learn that you're a human, and that these people in court are human.

Cherryhomes, with his outbursts and sarcasm, and Blenden, with his wise-cracking, saucy demeanor, became the spectacle on your behalf.

■ ■ ■

The sky above Roswell has gained a reputation. People come here to gawk celestially, to share stories of direct encounters without the condescending snicker they might draw back home. But Paul Bohannon, a twenty-four-year-old who found himself working in Chaves County as a car wreck litigator in 1979, had no patience for the insubstantial. His was a world of facts: speed limits and BACs, shattered bones and glass. He favored the dried ink on settlement checks to talk of little green men. Yet in the early morning hours of February 9, with snow flurries portending a storm, Bohannon found himself standing alone on the tarmac of Roswell Airfield watching a single light drop down out of the sky and hover above him.

The light came closer; after dipping beneath the clouds it materialized into a silver machine of noise and propulsion. Landing gear skidded on the runway. The turboprop blew Bohannon's coat open. He was temporarily blinded by the taxi lights. When the plane came to a stop and the boarding door swung open, a man scuttled onto the tarmac. He had on an expensive pair of cowboy boots but carried no luggage. He was heavyset and balding, which gave him the appearance of a man much older than his twenty-seven years. He spotted Bohannon, froze a moment, and then approached. "He shook my hand and introduced himself," Bohannon recalls. "But I didn't give a shit. I was worried about harboring a criminal."

The man was named Gary Dru Williams. It was Bohannon's job to usher him seventy-two miles south, past two counties' worth of law enforcement roadblocks set up explicitly to capture Williams, a fugitive in an arson case that was gaining, at least locally, a fair deal of attention.

Bohannon knew hardly anything else about the man or his case. "And I wanted it to remain that way. Hear no evil, see no evil. I took him to my car and had him change into a suit and a bolo tie. Then I handed him a blanket and told him to cover himself with it. He got down on the back seat floorboard of my Chevette. I said, 'Don't say another word to me until we're in Carlsbad.'"

Roswell's downtown is quaint to the point of banal, or would be, if not for what occurred in 1947. Where you'd expect to find a hardware store or a pharmacy you find instead the International UFO Museum and Research Center. On any given day, this town of forty thousand is swamped with desperate believers, conspiracy theorists, hucksters, self-published pamphleteers. The streetlamps have alien eyes painted on them. Bohannon's Chevette entered downtown before daybreak beneath the irradiated faces of these outré and glib-looking creatures. They stared down at him and the man who hid in the back seat.

Bohannon drove without the radio on. He'd never cared so scrupulously about his speedometer. Thankfully, the town was largely empty of activity except for newspaper deliverymen packing their cars. That morning the Associated Press headlined: "Pro-Shah Troops Attack Air Force Training Center. The UPI: Inflation Gallops Again in Jan." A front-page lede in the *Santa Fe New Mexican* announced President Jimmy Carter's new low in popularity polls, and a writer for the *Los Angeles Times* reported the largest monthly increase in the price of veal in national history. It was a typical Friday for that year, for the era. Only hours earlier, Paul had been sharing a warm bed with his wife in the quaint house they rented. Now, however, nothing seemed typical or quaint. Every sign—every gesture or change in the wind—spoke to the young lawyer of a massive shift in fate, as though he were crossing an invisible line that separated a promising attorney from the malefactors he represented.

It'd begun around three that morning, when a phone call awakened him. The call was from Dick Blenden, down in Carlsbad. Blenden was drunk.

"I need your help," he said. "Real weird situation down here. I got a kid coming in from Belize on a private jet. I need you to pick him up."

For Bohannon, car wreck litigation is a good gig in New Mexico, a state with one of the highest drunk driving incidences in the nation. While rushing from county to county and winning unwinnable cases, he'd caught the eye of older attorneys—especially Blenden, who kept a DUI lawyer on rolodex.

Through slurred but intelligent speech, Blenden laid out his predicament: down in Carlsbad, two high-profile businessmen had tried to burn down a commercial laundry to collect on the insurance. The scheme had failed and the men had been arrested, along with a son. All three now faced charges of attempted arson. Blenden felt he could get the charges lessened or even dropped, but the son had panicked and absconded to Belize.

Bohannon recalls: "Dick said that because both Gary Williams and his father were being charged as co-conspirators, the court could use the flight of the son as evidence of guilt against his father. He said the son was prepared to surrender, but the kicker was it had to be voluntary, and in court. If he were captured by police beforehand, Blenden wouldn't be able to avoid the flight implication." In other words, this kid Gary had to appear inside the courthouse and surrender before being spotted and arrested, and that meant by highway patrol, town cops, the bailiffs working inside the courthouse, the metal detector guys. Anybody.

Dick was asking Paul to harbor a wanted man and transport him for roughly ninety minutes, at which point he was to present the fugitive inside a packed courthouse—all by 7:30 that morning, and all without being stopped.

Paul said he'd take the job. "I was worried about the whole thing, but I knew Dick was a good guy. I trusted him. Probably a very stupid move."

It is a straight shot, an easy drive. Main Street in Roswell is merely a short stretch of US Route 285, which connects the Texas panhandle to Denver. Once you've passed Alien Invasion: T-Shirts and More!, you are left with flat chip-seal dragging out into a desert spotted only with bunch-grass and ocotillo. The pair left Roswell without coming upon a roadblock. This alleviated Bohannon only slightly. He kept his eyes west, watching a blizzard that was developing itself into a tight, purpling fist. He didn't want to outpace the storm and risk being pulled over, but he couldn't be stranded in the storm with a fugitive.

Nonetheless, the highway before them looked clear of traffic. Bohannon sighed and eased his grip on the wheel. He couldn't believe the luck. While he drove, he vaguely recalled reading about the crime in the paper. At first it'd been a small column, perhaps six lines, filed under "Courtroom News." But Bohannon had kept an eye on the story, thanks to how strange the circumstances were—how out of the ordinary the whole ordeal seemed.

Thirty miles south of Roswell, as the Chevette entered the small oil town of Artesia, Bohannon heard a disembodied voice call out from beneath the blanket.

"Hey, man. I'm hungry."

"I don't care if you're hungry. Just shut up and stay back there."

"You don't get it. I've got to have something before you take me into that courtroom. They're going to take me to jail and who knows when they'll feed me. I've got to have something to eat."

Dick Blenden had told Paul Bohannon not to stop, but the Williams kid had a point. An entire day or two could pass before the jailers would feed him.

Bohannon acquiesced. He turned the car off the main road and into the parking lot of an Allsup's.

As it happened, this particular convenience store was known for having the best coffee for miles. Naturally, then, the place was teeming with cops. Paul hesitated at the door but went inside, anyway. He nodded at a few patrolmen but the patrolmen were too busy chatting. He listened as he shopped. "I grabbed a sausage deal or something and either a Diet Coke or a cup of coffee. I can't remember: my mind was elsewhere." The cops were talking about the roadblocks and about the storm clouds. They were wondering how long it'd be until they'd get word that the threat of a blizzard had passed so they could 10-72.

Bohannon paid and left. He watched the rearview, absolutely believing he'd see blue lights soon. Another miracle. Nobody followed them. And the snowstorm looked to have puttered out somewhere near Picacho. The air was cold but the sky clear with the sun now opening itself over in Texas.

But Bohannon felt worse than ever: sensing the slowing of the vehicle, Gary Williams panicked. He began a confession. "I've never been in trouble before. I'm not a bad dude."

"I don't care."

"My brother is in prison. I'm not anything like him. I'm a general manager at my father's store. I only did this because he told me it would be easy. He said he and Roger have gotten away with it before."

"I told you I don't give a shit about any of it."

And he didn't. The less Paul Bohannon knew, the better. Like most good lawyers, he had acquired the ability of willful deafness. Whatever else Williams might have told him that morning, Bohannon would not remember. He was happy, relieved, and somehow less anxious once the courthouse revealed itself.

It is, for a small town, a beautiful building. Made up of pale stucco and flat rooflines, and adorned by thin, tall piñon trees, the building harkened to the days of Spanish dominance. The interior had terrazzo floors, and the west-facing door was scarred with the region's most important cattle ranching brands. The double doors on the south side, the main entrance, were terrifically heavy and reinforced with iron. But it is not an original building; it holds no historical significance except for this: the original Eddy County Courthouse looked a bit like the Dakota Building—too Hessian and baroque. During the Depression, and with funding from the WPA, the building was torn down simply to give the unemployed something to do.

Perhaps it was a design flaw, or perhaps the result of government spending oversight, but Paul knew that the west and the south entrances were radically different. The south side, the ornate, public side, had bailiffs and metal detectors and all the facade of modern safety. The west-side entrance, hardly used, out near the dumpsters and utility vehicles, was wholly unguarded.

Here is Paul Bohannon's recollection of what happened next.

"We walked straight to the elevators and got on, and sure enough, here comes a cop. He gets on the elevator with us. I thought, 'Well, shit. We're going to get caught now.' Gary kept his head down. He had his coat open so you could see the suit. The cop didn't say anything. They were looking for Williams, but maybe they didn't know what he looked like.

"In any event, I thought, 'Boy, when this door opens, I bet there are—' And sure enough. The door opened onto the third floor and there were four or five police officers out there, just standing around, chatting."

Paul and Gary stood motionless inside the elevator. The group of cops turned and looked at them both. Something strange happened. "Maybe because we were in suits, or, most likely, a few of them knew who I was—in any event, they didn't stop us. They didn't think anything about us.

"I ushered Gary toward the courtroom. In Carlsbad, they have these big, heavy courtroom doors. The judge was Johnny Walker. I liked him, but he was a stickler for decorum. So, anyway, I threw open those courtroom doors. The case was just about ready to start. Judge Walker was going over preliminary information with the lawyers, who were all standing. Everything went silent. Walker just stared at us. I yelled at the top of my voice, 'Judge Walker? We're here to surrender!' The judge was absolutely shocked. Everybody was shocked. But no sooner did I say who Gary was, and three cops ran over and grabbed his ass."

For Paul Bohannon, that was the end of the story. He was allowed to leave Carlsbad later that morning, making it back home in time for lunch. A decade later, he moved to Texas and joined a leading global energy law firm. As partner he settled more than $1 billion in claims on behalf of energy pipeline and chemical concerns. Today he co-owns a large sports memorabilia business. "When I tell people that story," he said to me after, chuckling, "they hardly believe it. Everybody says it sounds like the plot to a movie or something. It's the strangest thing I've ever done in my career. I can't believe I went through with it." It makes for a fabulous cocktail anecdote, one of youthful folly told by a man with an august career.

■ ■ ■

Bond hearings are short affairs. For crimes such as DUI, it is rare for a defendant to even appear. They can last as little as a few minutes and typically no longer than an hour, since it is customary for the state and for the defense to have hammered out some rough agreement ahead of the actual hearing.

According to Jim O'Hearn, writing for the *Current-Argus*, Dubb and Roger's hearing was a "marathon" that lasted nearly thirteen hours. "The hearing started at 9 a.m. There was less than an hour break for lunch, and testimony ran steadily until 11 p.m." Eighteen witnesses took the stand. O'Hearn continued, "Friday's preliminary often turned into a loud exchange between defense attorney Tom Cherryhomes, representing Williams, and assistant district attorney Wes Bobbitt. The two attorneys, and Dick Blenden, counsel for Jenkins, were called into [the judge's] chambers several times for consultation during the arguments."

This was precisely the chaos Dubb Williams and Roger Jenkins had paid for. Even a bond hearing would be a battle of attrition. No detail would be too minute. When a witness at the hearing said he'd found green canisters meant to hold gas, Cherryhomes pressed: Was the witness certain the canisters were green and not orange? Was the witness perhaps colorblind? There were arguments over who owned keys to which doors and which former employees might have still held keys; arguments over how alarm systems worked and who had access to them from home. A witness for the prosecution stated that in the months leading up to the arson, Roger Jenkins had spent an inordinate amount of time at Gibson's. This was countered by another witness who pointed out that it had been the holiday season, and Jenkins, in his ever civic-mindedness, often bought frozen turkeys and handed them out to the poor. One of Jenkins's employees stated that he'd seen the octane booster hidden beneath mops and tarps at least two days before the burning. Another, who'd closed shop the night of the 12th, stated that he'd never seen anything of the sort. Nearly everybody in the courtroom stated that they'd had a call from Roger Jenkins in the days preceding, claiming to be on his way to Tennessee; as Dick Blenden pointed out, at no time did any law enforcement official follow up on his alibi. Evening settled in. Carlsbad's prominent, now off from work, filled the spectator pews. A simple bond hearing was turning into a full-blown trial—a circus.

Shockingly, the state, who'd been so adamant that Gary Dru Williams appear in court, decided not to call him to the stand. Tom Cherryhomes did. He saw the state's decision to avoid Gary as a flaw in their armor and capitalized on it. "The younger Williams," wrote O'Hearn, "testified that his father had been in El Paso on store business and he [Gary] had asked him [Dubb] to buy the octane booster while there. He said he wanted it for his racing car . . . Gary Williams said he took the fuel to O'Neal Motors (where the car was housed) and placed it in his racing car. He said he hid it under a tarpaulin, but someone later 'ripped off' his car. He said the thief took the fuel, and other auto parts including a tachometer and a carburetor. He said he had not seen the cans of fuel since . . . " Confusingly, improbably, there is no evidence of anybody asking Gary Williams why he'd left Carls-bad for Belize after the arrests. The issue that'd brought Paul Bohannon to the brink of jeopardizing his career was no longer an issue at all. These kinds of turns, where lives are on the line and then suddenly not, are only baffling to those who have not tangled with our legal system. An accused can move from "facing two to ten years in the penitentiary" to writing a check for a fine. Attorneys hell-bent on the appearance of a witness might, within days, find the witness no longer needed or even anathema to their new narrative. And trials are nothing other than narrative.

Gary was finally formally called to appear late in the evening. Closing arguments soon followed. Dick Blenden called the whole affair a miscar-riage of justice. That Roger Jenkins had been made a suspect at all was a travesty. The only facts tying him to the case were that he owned the Steam Laundry and that he knew Dubb. Cherryhomes spoke afterward and mirrored Blenden's feelings. He added that he believed the DA wouldn't have the guts to continue, but if they did, it ought to be a warning to the populace. "Anyone in town could be bound over for a crime." Exasperated, annoyed, tired, Judge Walker closed the hearing where it had begun, leav-ing bond for each defendant at $10,000. The arson charge was dropped, as were the conspiracy charges that'd led Gary to flee the country. These charges were replaced with the lesser crime of attempted arson. Blenden and Cherryhomes had done their jobs.

The actual trial lasted four months, with motions filed and dismissed. Blenden and Cherryhomes managed to have the presiding judge recuse himself. Once the verdict came, under Judge Edward Snead, it was late June. And then it was September 11, 1979, and both men were home.

In contrast, Gary's trial was largely ignored by both the local press and the local citizenry. His father and Roger's bond hearing received over ten columns in the local paper; Gary's was given a short paragraph under "Court News" in the back pages. According to the criminal complaint: "On June 13, 1979, FBI Fingerprint expert Bob Witt told Lt. Tully by long distance telephone that he had identified palm and fingerprints of Gary Williams as those on Can #2 of the Moroso Octane Booster and also from the Hudson sprayer." The complaint also notes the presence of a tennis shoe print, "the sole pattern of which contains circles and diamonds," throughout the premises. "[This led] Lt. Sadler to believe that the person wearing the shoe stepped into the liquid that left the residue trail and then out onto the clean area of the floor. The print was near the back door, the northeast room [Roger Jenkins's office] and also matched a print located just outside the back door." The design matched Gary's shoes.

On the stand, Gary told the court he could not have been involved in the arson attempt because he was not in Carlsbad. Rather, he'd gone first to Dallas, Texas, and then to Albuquerque, driving a race car he owned. Later, at O'Neal Motors, Gary discovered that, along with a carburetor and tachometer, the fuel additive found to have been used in the arson had been stolen from his car. But Jerry Owens, the service manager at O'Neal Motors and "personal friend of the defendant" could not substantiate this. Gary's testimony was deemed "false or improbable." In all, the trial lasted four days. A guilty verdict was handed down on January 26, 1980, mere hours after closing statements. Gary was convicted of attempted arson. The sentence was probated. Judge Snead sent him to Old Main for a sixty-day diagnostic—just as he had Roger and Dubb.

But, of course, nothing like Roger and Dubb. Nothing like them at all.

∎ ∎ ∎

The arson attempt had been poorly considered, shambolic in its undertaking, and largely of no consequence. All were found guilty but given probated sentences. At the time, this order demanded a sixty-day

44

commitment to the maximum security prison in Santa Fe for "diagnostic evaluation."

Dubb and Roger Jenkins began their stint in June 1979. By then, the Penitentiary of New Mexico had a reputation for its harsh conditions, but the December escape had yet to wake the public to the true systemic barbarity inside. When the two middle-aged white businessmen returned to Carlsbad on September 11, their reactions were like children after an ineffective paddling. Dubb, grinning, told folks he was a new man. Roger, also joking, was keen to say: "The only crime you may find me guilty of from here on out is over-tithing to the church." Their impression of Old Main had been limited to the admissions and orientation dormitory, where Gary was headed. The men held there were similar to them, or else so poor as to not cover the simplest of bond before a court appearance. Over the course of their short time in A&O, Dubb and Roger had been occluded from the harsh realities of the other wings and cellblocks of the prison. To them, Old Main was a place to sit in the corner for having been a bad citizen. You were free to wear your own clothing, and on weekends the TV room stayed open until 1:30 in the morning. There were games of cards and, of course, the radios. The food wasn't so good, but the rest of it felt something akin to a really bad resort. Once Gary's sentence came down in January 1980, both his father and Roger assured the much-younger Gary his time at PNM would be insignificant, and when he came out, they would make certain he had a positive future awaiting him.

This advice had to have lost all of its comfort by the time Gary was escorted from the Eddy County jail to the transit van. The governor's response to the escape had been to rely on the bureaucracy that had failed in the first place. Gary, passing Charles Martin's ranch, passing the cold and barren landscape as the sun rose and turned what remained of the dark northern counties from an abstraction into a beautifully haunting reality, must have looked for something to bolster his confidence. But if the words of his father and Roger, of the governor and the state, offered any comfort at all, that balm would only last a few hours longer. Gary Williams's trip from Eddy County to the sally port at the PNM occurred on February 1, 1980. By two o'clock that morning, the walls of the prison were awash in blood.

CHAPTER THREE

The Penitentiary of New Mexico, the first, and at the time only, maximum-security institution in the state, occupied 640 acres of state land situated about fourteen miles south of Santa Fe. It sat on the western side of the Madrid Highway, which leads down out of the Sangre de Cristo Mountains to the ghost town of Golden and then splits into two separate roads, each of which end in dire places, one known as Edgewood and the other, to the west, has no name at all. If you are a farmer, the Madrid Highway is fortuitous in getting your crops to the main markets, but there's no reason for anybody else to travel this particular route unless they are a convicted felon.

The complex was painted a pinkish-brown and sat squat, relying on professional landscaping to add contrast; in its earliest iterations, a new inmate entering Old Main from the outside was met with an institution, according to John R. Curtis of the *Albuquerque Tribune*, "beautifully situated amid green-clad hills rolling away to picturesque mountains in the distance. . . . The buildings are trim, modern and attractive, and inside the double-fence [the penitentiary] is surrounded by velvety lawns and a few trees and shrubs all groomed to the superlative degree." Inside, the design relied heavily on Alfred Hopkins's work at the Lewisburg Federal Penitentiary in Pennsylvania, which had opened two decades earlier. This sort of architecture broke from the two common models of the day: the brutal chain gang agricultural prisons of the Deep South, and the labyrinthine Big Houses, such as Sing-Sing in the Northeast, where prisoners virtually disappeared into the enormity of the facility. Using the telephone pole design, Old Main consisted of one long central corridor running south to north with wings of cellblocks, dormitories, the cafeteria, a hospital, and a gymnasium branching out to the east and west. Because PNM was the only institution of its size in the state, the telephone pole design promised to keep certain classifications of inmates—from probation violators to informants to murderers—apart. The grilles to each wing were controlled electronically from a central command unit, positioned at the halfway point of the main hallway. The central office stuck out into the main hallway like a nub on a tree trunk; behind its waffle-coned glass and iron, guards kept an eye on all goings-on and passed keys to officers via a small slot. A main grille separated the north wing from the south—the north wing would hold the fiercest of inmates, while the south would offer less violent inmates protection.

Of course, first-time inmates had an altogether different greeting of the institution than did visitors. Sometime late in the afternoon of February 1, Gary Williams's transit van pulled into the sallyport near the kitchen. The first impressions, then, were not of landscaping but of mechanical grilles, electronic doors, the slamming of steel on steel. The brutal honesty of reinforced concrete. The ceilings were low, perhaps ten feet high. The central corridor was loud, incessantly loud, and the ceilings did not help with the noise from the much taller and spacy cellblocks, and they did not help with the weather. Old Main was not air-conditioned, nor was it heated. This is common in Santa Fe, where the weather rarely strays from room temperature. When it does, however, it is usually in the winter, and at an elevation of nearly eight thousand feet above sea level, both winds off of the plains and blizzards from the Rockies can drop temperatures drastically.

To combat this, Gary and the other newbies arriving at PNM that day were given navy blue beanies and coveralls marked A&O. They were corralled into the Protestant chapel. There, they bit into their first of the notorious bologna sandwiches. They ate and sat silent. Through the corridor, through the echoes, they heard shouting from the north side, shouting and cursing and radios and threats and so must've been happy to have been escorted to the much quieter south side.

For reasons still unclear, the duty fell to the Protestant chaplain to finish the brief education these young men received about their new lives, where the code was far different than it was on the streets. "Many of the fellas have gotten right with God in here," Reverend Bolan often said, focusing on ideals rather than praxis. "There's about eight fellas out in the ministry today, and they got started in here. So . . ."

He ended with: "Don't serve time. Make time serve you."

After this less than scholastic orientation, the newcomers were marched to the far south end of the prison, to dormitory D-1. Protocol had inmates stand in single file against the wall of the corridor while officers checked the latest roster sheet. The A&O unit held men popped for petty crimes—kids, mostly, with drug problems. Many of them would soon be relocated to either small county jails or to the much-beloved Farm in Los Lunas.

A&O was not without its troubles. The dorm, meant to house fifty men, already held eighty-six, and as the new arrivals filed inside, it became clear that all of the bunks had been claimed. Officers had inmates sleep between the bunks, on the concrete floor. But those spaces were soon filled, too. Officers could not let it get so bad as to have an inmate sleep in a shower stall, so they decided to choose one new inmate to lock up in Cellblock Four. Just for the night. By following this ersatz line of thinking, they noticed, too, that a name had been added late to the roster: James Bunch, by coincidence also from Eddy County. Due to alphabetical order, the inmate moved to Cellblock Four would've been Gary Dru Williams. Instead, they took Bunch.

None of this mattered to Williams or to Bunch, who weren't familiar with the penitentiary's classification system. The reasoning given to them for the move was that both places were heavily protected; that it was merely for the evening; and that Cellblock Four, like A&O, had television rights that night until 1:30 a.m. Bunch likely shrugged and went along.

For the men who remained inside A&O that night, your best option was to try your hand at blending in and perhaps chatting with the crowd watching television. Find somebody to watch your back.

Gary had something else on his mind: his brother, Jeffrey Lloyd Williams, was housed here already—in a different dorm and under different circumstances.

CHAPTER FOUR

Debra Sibley was a barrel racer. She and her husband, W. C., owned a Holiday Rambler mini motorhome and traveled the country—Debra working the rodeo circuit while her husband worked as a general manager for a company called National Alethes. This was in early August 1976. They were young, two years into their marriage, and loved the nomadic lifestyle. They traveled upward of eighty thousand miles each year. When W. C. broke his ankle that summer, the couple drove home to Carlsbad and parked the motorhome in his parents' double-car driveway. It was time to relax and take it easy, at least for a bit. This was the perfect place to do just that: W. C.'s mother was a doting woman. She made the couple meals; washed, dried, and ironed their laundry; and if a phone call came, she was quick to fetch the young couple. She didn't mind long-distance charges.

The couple stayed in the Rambler's loft bedroom rather than inside the Sibley house. The Rambler was their home and the mattress was agreeable, and while the temperature during the days crested over one hundred degrees, they could go inside and watch the television and wait for the cool desert nights, which were lovely.

On the night of August 6, Debra went to bed before W. C. He stayed up with his parents to watch the CBS Friday Night Movie. Around 1:30 W. C. hobbled out of the house and through the garage toward the motorhome. He couldn't close the garage door; he was in too much pain. He left it open, not thinking much of it. W. C. was a deep sleeper, so he did not wake when, an hour after coming to bed, somebody pulled on the Rambler's door.

The trailer rocked. Debra woke. "When the motorhome rocked, [I] looked out the window thinking it was [W. C.'s mother]." She didn't see her mother-in-law. She didn't see anybody. Debra soon realized something was odd. "Under the streetlight was parked a Blazer-looking vehicle with the door open and it was just sitting there." She waited. Somebody yanked on the door again. "It felt like somebody was trying to rip the door off the hinges, is what it felt like." She looked out of the curtain again and saw that somebody was sitting behind the steering wheel of the Blazer.

W. C. woke up. "What the hell's going on?" When W. C. looked outside, he saw no car under the streetlight. "They're gone," he said, and yawned and put his head back down on his pillow.

"No, they're not," Debra said.

The Blazer had moved. It was no longer across the street. Rather, it was parked directly in front of the Rambler, its bumper nearly up against the home's towing rig. Debra cracked open the window. "Can I help you?" she shouted. A young man sprinted out of the garage. "He was blond-headed and slight of build and he had like a T-shirt on—a white T-shirt and jeans." It happened so fast she couldn't tell if the blond kid was holding anything. She watched him dive inside the Blazer's open passenger door. The vehicle took off.

The Sibley couple went inside and Debra and her mother-in-law spoke to the police by phone, while W. C. and his father went out into the garage to look around. Sure enough, the old man's pickup was open and the CB radio had been pulled out, leaving only some wiring behind. His deer rifle was gone, too.

Carlsbad police officer Eddie Carrasco arrived soon after and took the report. He didn't tell the Sibleys that only an hour earlier another call had come from an apartment complex less than a mile south. Another stolen CB, and the witness had a similar description of the vehicle and suspect. Before he left he told the family to stay calm and indoors. He told them he and his partner would be on the lookout for the vehicle. He asked them not to hesitate if they had any further information to relay to the police.

Not long after Carrasco left, W. C. told Debra he couldn't sleep; he wanted to go out looking for the perpetrator. The shock had worn off. Now he felt violated and angry. His father's rifle was a family keepsake. Not an heirloom, per se, but still important to the Sibleys. It was a Ruger M77 with a Weaver V9-V scope mounted to it. Moreover, Mr. Sibley had had it customized: he'd had a diamond engraved into the bottom side of the trigger guard and, beneath the diamond, the letter C engraved with a slash through it. This represented an old Carlsbad cattle brand.

Debra agreed with her husband. Neither she nor W. C. were the type of people to be assuaged by a police officer's words. They weren't the type to take something lying down.

They took a pickup and drove around. They headed south of the Pecos River. It was very early in the morning, approaching three, but was a Friday in August; a lot of high school kids without curfews and college kids home for the summer were shooting the drag. Every town had some form of the drag. The phrases are different, but the concept was universal. In Carlsbad, you "shot the drag" because you had absolutely nothing else to do, but you had a driver's license. In Carlsbad, the drag began down on the banks of the Pecos River, not far from President's Park, an amusement park with a patriotic bent. From there you passed Lakeside Meats and the enormous cow on its roof, up Canal, beyond the pharmacies and the baroque county courthouse, the Western wear store, the BBQ restaurant, the football stadium, and finally ending at Becky's Drive-In. Becky's was the beginning of a new loop: ride back to the banks of the river, or call it an evening and find a mesa party out east, or head to the make-out spot in the aptly named Happy Valley.

Around 3:30 that morning, Debra spotted a Blazer coming out of the parking lot of O'Neal Motors on Pierce Street.

"That's it," she said.

"Are you sure?"

"Absolutely."

W. C. followed the car to a stoplight. He pulled up next to the Blazer. He was fuming, but Debra told him to play it cool. W. C.'s left ankle was busted, and anyway, the rifle that'd been stolen was loaded.

W. C. said to the driver: "Hey, man. What's going on tonight?" This language surprised Debra. "My husband and I rodeo. We're cow people. We don't use that kind of language." She'd never heard W. C. say, "Hey, man" to anybody. "But these people appeared to be that sort, so he just used what he thought was their language." She later clarified, calling it "hippie talk."

The driver, who had dark hair, and the passenger, the blond guy Debra had seen running from the garage, laughed. The blond guy smiled. "Not much, man. Just driving around, trying to get drunk."

Debra later told Officer Eddie Carrasco, "The blond-headed boy looked to me like he was a little more than drunk. Like he was either on drugs or that he was spaced out or that he didn't really give a darn about anything. He wasn't sloppy like you are when you're under the influence of alcohol. He just thought he was really cool, and his speech was real slow."

But Debra also had a pang of self-doubt. The passenger was dressed the same as the guy she saw leaving the garage. And the car was the same.

But looking at the blond guy now, he looked older, at least a decade older. As Debra put it: "The report I gave to the officer was that he was slight of build and that he looked like he was about nineteen and when we saw him in the Blazer he looked like he was thirty or older. You know, he just looked—from the slight of build that—from the way he looked from behind—he looked a lot older, looking at him in the face."

The blond guy said, "The cops just stopped us and hassled us about stealing a bunch of stuff."

Now his grin looked more sophisticated, more acerbic, than Debra had given the blond man credit for. What a thing to say. W. C. clenched his teeth and tightened his fists on the steering wheel. He took a moment before saying, "Well, if there's nothing going on, we'll see you later."

The men in the Blazer laughed and sped away.

Back home and incensed, Debra called Officer Eddie Carrasco and told him that they'd seen the two burglars near O'Neal's. It was now nearing 4:30 in the morning. Two hours had passed. Before Carrasco and his partner had made it to Pierce Street, they spotted the Blazer themselves at a Circle K. It was abandoned, but the plates came back to a twenty-year-old named Charles Hubert Barnes. Barnes had no real criminal history but he was known to spend a lot of time with his neighbor, Jeffrey Lloyd Williams, a blond twenty-year-old widely known to law enforcement in at least four southern New Mexico counties.

It isn't difficult to understand Debra Sibley's doubts in her physical description of Jeff Williams. The facts are fairly simple and average. He was born on July 1, 1956, a month before his older brother Gary turned four. He was five-foot-nine, slender. He had a wispy mustache, or else a mustache made less substantial by its light color. My father, who grew up around Jeff, thought him ugly. Girls thought he had pretty blue eyes and long eyelashes. This tempered the hardened West Texas dialect.

Jeff Williams liked to race. He liked to go fast. He was thirteen when first pulled over for a driving infraction. By sixteen, Jeff had been cited or arrested nearly two dozen times: careless driving, speeding, reckless driving, fleeing or eluding police, driving without a license, two collisions. Each of these cases were adjudicated, dropped, or resulted in minor fines and perhaps some light reform. The judges, many of them, were Goldcoaters. They listened to Dubb talk about his two boys. It was clear who was off-limits, and Dubb was often open to hearing all sorts of compromises.

No sooner had Jeff been arrested for the theft than he was back out, shooting the drag in his '76 Monte Carlo. "It bothered a lot of people," my mother said. She was born around the same time and into the same social class as Williams. Her father ran the Chamber of Commerce, which sponsored the Goldcoaters. "A lot of kids with means could get away with a lot of misdemeanors that might've caused real trouble for a regular kid. So I can't cast aspersions (though my mother swears she never did wrong), but I think everybody in town, the kids I mean, we just thought there was something very different with the Williamses. It wasn't simple, stupid stuff. Even by high school, the stuff Jeff was up to was bordering on the dangerous."

Jeff did nothing halfway. College, forget about it. He wasn't going. The best open roads in the world were right here. From Carlsbad to Odessa, the old Jal Highway is a straight two-lane used only by potash trucks. And there is US 62, which can take a driver from Carlsbad down to El Paso and into Juarez, the drag a lovely lonesome place at night, the nights incredibly dark save for the stars and the distant fires from the tops of refinery flare stacks and the wild, panicked eyes of jackrabbits and desert shrews. And, of course, there is Highway 285 to the capital city. Jeff had no interest in the world beyond these roads. He could be free here. He could be free to go fast. Sometimes he went so fast he felt his head would implode. To come down, he took Demerol, and lots of it. The drug is an opioid analgesic, not dissimilar to morphine. The FDA's description of Demerol is nine pages long and almost completely given over to warnings, precautions, adverse reactions, and contraindications. It shares a Schedule II with the likes of Dilaudid, fentanyl, codeine, methadone, and OxyContin, as well as stimulants such as Dexedrine and methamphetamine hydrochloride. Some patients experience a high similar to cocaine, which is to say, Demerol is a legal speedball.

Around daybreak of that August morning in 1976, Eddie Carrasco, back in his office, received a phone call from a tipster. It was Charles Barnes's mother, Judy. She told the police that if they were to search her property, they were likely to find stolen goods.

The case was in the bag, and so Officer Carrasco, with the gumshoe work over, was joined ceremoniously by Sergeant Jim Bogle and Captain Ralph Freeman—to arrest a young man at his mother's house. While Charles, hungover, stood by, Judy Barnes directed the police to different closets and cubbies. Finally, Charles Barnes told them where to look: a storage shed in the backyard. Behind a drop cloth, the three officers found the Sibley rifle and the two stolen CBs.

The next morning, Charles Barnes woke up completely sober and inside the Eddy County jail. He told police he wanted a plea bargain. For a lesser charge, Barnes agreed to testify against Jeff Williams. This was more than satisfying to the Carlsbad Police Department. By 1976, at the age of twenty, Jeff Williams had become such a disturbance that in open court and under direct examination, Captain Ralph Freeman admitted once to his desire to see Jeff sent to state prison.

> Q: Have you ever made a statement to the effect that you would like to see [Jeff Williams] placed in the state penitentiary?
> FREEMAN: I did, yes.
> Q: Do you recall if it was made here in Carlsbad?
> FREEMAN: Yes, sir.
> Q: Was it to more than one person? Is that why you don't recall who it was made to?
> FREEMAN: I don't recall making any more than one statement.
> Q: Do you recall what you said?
> FREEMAN: Not the exact words. I did say that he was involved in a lot of stuff and if I could send him to the penitentiary I would.

■ ■ ■

The initial charges had Jeff facing two separate one-to-five-year sentences at the Penitentiary of New Mexico, and, by the testimony of the acting captain, had law enforcement actively pursuing any route that would see Jeff imprisoned. On his side, however, was Dubb and his influence.

Jeff's father hired a young Hollywood-actor-handsome attorney named Tom Cherryhomes. Cherryhomes had been a college baseball player, was six-foot-four, and was a master at defense work. He had Jeff's first trial judge disqualified. He put the trial off for nearly a year. Later, when cross-examining Debra Sibley, he managed to upset her composure by asking her about a car wreck and insurance claim that'd occurred in California and had not gone in her favor.

SIBLEY: I think a lot of the law enforcement. If it wouldn't have been for them I probably wouldn't be here.

CHERRYHOMES: You like law enforcement but you don't like defense attorneys.

SIBLEY: No, I like defense attorneys fine but I think you're obnoxious.

CHERRYHOMES: Thank you.

SIBLEY: You're welcome.

CHERRYHOMES: To me that's the highest compliment you can ever pay me.

SIBLEY: I guess that's your job.

THE COURT: Let's get on with it.

Finally on October 11, 1977, Jeff Williams received a probated sentence—as had Charles Barnes. Nobody in town had been surprised by Jeff grinning during a trial that could end with him spending his twenties behind bars. He knew, long before the verdict, how this whole incident would end.

CHAPTER FIVE

Around the time his brother Jeff was raising hell and gaining notoriety for it, Gary Dru Williams, now twenty-four, tried to stay on the straight and narrow. While flipping through a magazine one afternoon, he found an advertisement for the National School of Meat Cutting in Toledo, Ohio.

> Train quickly in 8 short weeks at Toledo for a bright future with security in the vital meat business. Big pay, full-time jobs—HAVE A PROFITABLE MARKET OF YOUR OWN! Pay after graduation. Diploma given. Job help. Thousands of successful graduates. Our 41st year!

Gary filled out the application and sent a $250 check. Not so long after, an acceptance letter arrived. To date, this had been Gary Williams's biggest accomplishment. He'd never been as proud of himself as he was reading that letter. That hot August in 1976, while Jeff was out with Charles Barnes, Gary Williams daydreamed of owning his own butcher shop. It was Gary's way out of the shadow of his brother. He knew nothing of Toledo, so he let himself imagine it in the kindest of terms.

He arrived with a lot of hope and a few things packed into one suitcase. Those first few days away from home were an epiphany. Here there was grass and rain and taxis and honking. Things he'd seen on sitcoms but had never seen before with his own eyes.

However, the excitement, the feeling of renewal, only lasted until classes were underway. Gary felt out of touch. This was not a certificate easily granted. They took meat seriously here. The institute had twenty-four-page packets combined in a twenty-five-packet volume: a six-hundred-page, leather-bound tome with your name embossed on the lower left-hand corner of the cover, and you were expected to know every word of every packet, every illustration, and to pass a two-part comprehensive exam before coming remotely close to handling a knife. The textbooks taught you subjects such as "Grading Pork for Pricing and Display" and "Lamb, Mutton, and Veal Management," and "Rendering Poultry: How to Advertise." And later there were the knife classes, the classes on band saws, the three-cornered block scraper, the larding needle and oil stone. There was a science and an art, a panache, to meat. There was a specific Toledo Cut to a sirloin. You were expected to uphold the tradition.

The school was on the second and third floors of a building on Summit Street, above the Kurtz Meat Market. Kurtz had enormous neon signs along its facade. It looked like a casino. THIS IS KURTZ, the central sign read. The others showed the day's price of neck bones and wiener sausages. The market was a promise: once you'd succeeded academically, you could put on an apron and greet the public downstairs.

Gary had come here because he faltered in traditional academic settings. He disliked the conceptual. He liked working with his hands and thought being a butcher was tactile. Yet he was finding himself in a kind of photo-negative of a competitive boarding school. The institute promoted meat cutting as a cerebral endeavor. That was another thing: to call somebody here a butcher was a grave insult. Gary found this out the hard way early into his tutelage. Butchers worked in slaughterhouses. Butchers worked with offal. Butchers hacked away at limbs and things. Nowhere in their literature did the Toledo school refer to their work as that of a butcher.

In December, the town placed holiday decorations on the buildings along Summit Street, but the winds off the Maumee River wreaked havoc on them. Gary wore a coat and a hat against the snowdrifts. Temperatures dipped into the teens and then the single digits. This happened back home, but back home the weather was almost always dry. In Toledo, Lake Erie sometimes acted up and dumped a godless chill onto the city.

He drank in the bars. He bought packs from cigarette machines. He looked for a girl. "You're funny," they'd say, and Gary's big cheeks would go red. *Urban Cowboy* was not out yet, but the cowboy thing should've worked for him. Waylon Jennings and Willie Nelson and the Outlaw Country scene around Austin was spreading across the hinterlands as an alternative to disco. When Gary heard their songs on the jukebox he'd sing along. He couldn't carry a tune. Leadbottom, the guys back home called him. "You're funny," the girls in Toledo would continue to say. But Gary's pearl-snap shirts came unsnapped around his gut, and often he was left alone at closing time to gather his shit—to put on his sheepskin jacket and hat.

At night, the city terrified him. He got lost often. Cowboy boots lack traction, and he'd slip on black ice. He liked the bus lines, though. He'd never in his life known public transportation. Sometimes he skipped his classes at the institute to ride in grand circles around the city, transferring when he felt like it. He could ride all day. From Ottawa Hills to Franklin Park all the way over to downtown Sylvania. He watched the lunchtime crowds give way to midafternoon winos, the elderly returning home from visiting deranged spouses way south of Airline Junction, at the psychiatric hospital. A bitter, uninspired evening snowfall would begin with flakes streaking down the bus windows, and the buses filled again at 4:30, at 5:00, with commuters looking haggard. They stood and sat in postures of minor misery. By the end of the commute, Gary could have fallen asleep with the last two chapters of *Facts About Beef* lying between his boots in the aisle.

After Cutting Test: Part One, a test he knew he had failed before receiving a grade, Gary purchased a bus ticket and returned to New Mexico. He'd never been so far away from home. He would never in his life venture this far again.

■ ■ ■

He reentered Carlsbad on a Trailways bus. He preferred not to talk to anybody, not to see anybody, but in order to find a place to stay he needed his parents to cosign on a lease. They did, and soon Gary had a mobile home in El Dorado Estates—3022 National Parks Highway, lot #79. From the tiny porch where he smoked cigarettes, Gary watched tourists leaving Carlsbad for the caverns, twenty miles south of town. He could also see across the barren land the Caverns City Air Terminal. On weekends, he watched his father's friends take off in their Cessnas, the tiny cabins filled with family or mistresses, the planes looping large around town before heading to the Guadalupes for the great views. Gary took a job working for his father. He was named general manager of the Gibson's discount store. Life was closing in on him. He had no girlfriend, no career, and now, in the mornings when he showered, his hair was falling out and clogging the drain.

During the first week of 1979, Roger Jenkins and Dubb Williams knocked on Gary's trailer door. They had a plan. It could give Gary a new chance at a future.

CHAPTER SIX

Sometime around midnight and into the early morning hours of February 2, 1980, snow began to fall in Santa Fe. It fell on the capitol grounds and along Paseo de Peralta and settled on the roof of the La Fonda hotel, on St. Francis Cathedral, and on the Allan Houser Sculpture Garden. And then the snow came in waves, piling up outside the Pink Adobe and La Casa Sena, outside the Bull Ring, a steakhouse near the capitol building where tourists and politicians finished glasses of wine while huddled near ancient fireplaces burning sweet-scented piñon wood. Snow fell in the deep, uninhabited valleys of the mountains and along the dried arroyos. It fell on the dark flat grounds of the penitentiary. That night quiet snowflakes found their way inside the institution from shattered windowpanes never repaired. Gary Dru Williams tried to adjust himself for sleep, his body against the bitterly cold floor of admissions and orientation.

Less than a half hour after the TV was turned off and the dayroom locked up, the dormitory awoke to mad, thundering howls from the corridor. "People were hooting and hollering, stampeding," an inmate from A&O later told a group of documentarians. "You'd have thought a bull had gotten loose in the corridor."

The men in A&O lacked context by which to judge this spontaneous eruption of noise. As another inmate described entering the sallyport for the first time: "Living in a dorm is like having your bunk set up in the middle of the San Diego Freeway." The televisions had been on late; inmates in E-2 had been partying. But this noise, this sudden and collective bellow, preceded by a hauntingly quiet half hour, sounded different.

The men in A&O soon had their fears confirmed. Officer Mike Hernandez, hardly an adult and with less than 120 days on the job, scrambled for the safety of the far south end. Before he could get his bearings, Officer Hernandez had locked himself inside the A&O dormitory with eighty-six inmates—the same dorm he had helped lock down only a half hour earlier. Mike Hernandez took a moment to gauge the situation before radioing Officer Lawrence Lucero in the control center. Hernandez's warning came minutes too late. Lucero had already heard the message, directly from the mouths of the men who'd started the unrest.

■ ■ ■

The night shift for February 2 began at midnight and was meant to run until 8:00 that morning. Officer Lawrence Lucero had begun working for corrections right after earning his GED; he was now twenty-three, but had only worked the prison's control center a few times. He was posted there to replace Officer Marcella Armijo, who had veteran experience inside the control center but had failed to show for work that night. Other decisions made by Captain Gregorio Roybal cannot be so quickly explained: Herman Gallegos, a correctional officer with twenty-six years of experience, was transferred for the night from his duties in Cellblock Four, the most vulnerable cellblock in the institution, to transportation detail. He spent the crucial opening hours before the takeover bringing back a low-security inmate from his nightly shift at the Palace House Restaurant in Santa Fe.

Perhaps it didn't matter. Following the December escape, Cellblock Five, which housed a majority of those inmates who'd broken free, was given the governor's approval to be renovated. Construction crews moved in, and the inmates in the block were transferred—many of them landing in dormitory E-2, a medium-security unit home to largely white-collar criminals. According to Danny Ray Macias, one of the hardened convicts moved from Cellblock Five to E-2, he and Alex Garcia had begun brewing liquor on January 28. They had a connection among the kitchen staff, and over time they'd cached a pound of raisins and four pounds of sugar. They poured these ingredients into a Hefty bag and added the squeezed juices of nearly a dozen citrus fruits. They added yeast and stored this in a pipe-chase until early on the evening of February 1. Macias later described what happened to State Police investigators assigned to postriot interviews by Attorney General Jeff Bingaman:

> So come Friday, February the first, we pulled out the home brew and it was . . . I guess it was the most potent batch that we had made cause we let it sit a long time; plus we had a lot of sugar and a lot of yeast, and that creates a lot of alcohol, and when I went up there to get it I brought it down and I opened it. . . . Ohhhh it's powerful stuff.
> We started drinking around 8:00. We drank till about 8:25; we stopped at 8:30 cause we knew the time [head count] was gonna be around any minute and we waited and sure enough around 8:35

the guards came in to count, and how they didn't smell that stuff is beyond me because it was the loudest-smelling stuff. God, it smelled like a brewery in there.

The [guards] just went about their business counting and took off outside. And we went back to the corner and were drinking. By that time I was pretty loaded. I had drank about three glasses and that stuff was plenty powerful. I was getting kinda high.

I was watching TV most of the night and Rudy Aldaz came and was talking with Alex and some other guys and Freddie Velasquez, the homeboy, we used to go to high school together. He came over and I told him, "Hey, remember that thing that I was telling you the other day, and that if you wanted showing in about the takeover?"

And he said, "Yeah."

"Well, we're gonna talk about it tonight. Why don't you come down. Si quieres, le ponemos. If you don't, well, that's all right, too."

I was pretty well drunk come one o'clock, because it was time to watch *Midnight Special*. Rudy Aldaz calls me over and he says, "Look. We've been talking and we're going to take over tonight." I laughed. I thought it was a joke.

Macias, Aldaz, and Garcia very quickly found themselves drinking with four Anglos from California—also Cellblock Five transfers. The mix inside E-2 was volatile: while most of the inmates housed there were fraudulent check writers or tax evaders—white-collar criminals trying to be granted early parole—their new neighbors were, most of them, looking at sentences between ten years and natural life. They were men with violent pasts and aggressive attitudes. Of the Anglos now housed in E-2, most of them comprised a group of former bikers and Aryan Brotherhood wannabes. They were Michael Price, the man who'd assisted Michael Colby and Jack Stephens in the baseball bat murder of another inmate; Thomas Dale Davis (Puppet); Wilfred LeBlanc (Frog); and Leo McGill. They expected little resistance by other inmates to their scheme that night. In fact, they threatened the others. According to Macias:

Alex banged on the table. This was around one o'clock. It woke some of the guys up and they looked at us, and Alex Garcia said, "Look here. We're gonna take over this motherfucking joint. If there's any one of you stupid motherfuckers that wants to get in my way and try to stop me. . . ." He hit the desk again with a piece of steel. "I'm gonna kill you."

Captain Gregorio Roybal met with the graveyard shift crew around 11:45; soon thereafter, outgoing officers dropped off their roll calls at the central command post, and the night shift officers performed the first of two head counts. The last one was slated for roughly 1:30 that morning. Roybal and his assistant shift commander, Lieutenant Joe Anaya, drank coffee in the officers' mess until 1:30 and left together to join Officers Michael Schmitt and Ronnie Martinez, who were beginning to lock down the dormitories on the southside of the pen.

The four of them went to B-1. There they reported nothing out of the ordinary. They left the unit and Lieutenant Anaya told Captain Roybal, "You have three people with you. I'll go to the A&O unit." Anaya joined Officer Mike Hernandez in locking Gary's unit down. They had no trouble. Lieutenant Anaya then noticed Officers Ronnie Martinez and Michael Schmitt joining Captain Roybal outside of B-2. Having just locked down that dorm, they were heading across the gangway to E-2.

Lieutenant Anaya told investigators he followed his fellow officers. There, the youngest of them, Ronnie Martinez, was left in charge of the door connecting the dormitory to the central corridor. Lieutenant Anaya followed Captain Roybal and Officer Schmitt into the dorm. This left Officer Ronnie Martinez with all sets of keys. Anaya took the right side of the central walkway with Officer Schmitt in front of him and Captain Roybal to his left. This was a violation of policy, as at no time during lockdown should the captain and his lieutenant be on the same side of the central corridor—to say nothing of being in the same dorm at the same time. Another violation of policy occurred when Officer Ronnie Martinez did not lock his fellow officers inside the dormitory during count. This was and still is standard procedure at every prison in the modern world: although the officers doing count are wholly cut off from the safety of fellow officers or SWAT involvement, the matter, how violent it may be, is contained to a single unit. But it was common at Old Main for young officers, too afraid or too uninformed, to disregard the protocol. There was yet a third violation that night: the emergency lights, a series of small blue night-lights lining the dormitory's rows, had shorted out over a month ago. In order for Officer Schmitt and Captain Roybal to effectively perform their duties, the officers walked into the darkness of a room housing sixty-two convicted felons. To put it another way: the math pits each officer against thirty-one inmates.

Danny Ray Macias described what happened next:

> Bueno, so. I was laying in my bed and I had been drinking a lot. I was getting dizzy. I looked up and I thought I was gonna throw up, and I looked up and I saw that the guards had turned off the lights in B-2. They were on their way this way. Everybody spread out and everybody was in position. And I was laying there and the fucking room was spinning on me. I was getting sick. I didn't think I was gonna make it. They got there before I threw up.
>
> Captain Roybal walked in on one side and Schmitt through the other. About five or ten seconds later, here comes Lieutenant Anaya. I looked around and when I did, Mike Price hit the door. I got up real fast and I tripped and I fell and I tripped and I damn near ran into the wall. And I finally got ahold of the officer as he was trying to get away and I had an axe in my hand that was Mike Price's and the officer was telling me not to kill him, and I said, "Nobody's gonna get hurt."

■ ■ ■

Before Lieutenant Anaya could respond, Rudy Aldaz and Alex Garcia, along with LeBlanc and McGill, carried the guards into the dayroom at the far western end of the dorm—an area that was farthest from the front door and had its own, separate grille. Despite Danny Macias's claims to authorities that he wanted to provide the officers with warmth and safety—offering that, under his command, other inmates supplied their new hostages with sheets and blankets for the cold—Macias does not deny that the officers were all stripped, blindfolded, and handcuffed. Nor does he go into detail about exactly what happened to the officers before they were offered blankets.

Lieutenant Anaya refuted Macias's testimony. "I walked back toward the grille and somebody pulled a knife on me. At this time they pulled the knife I tried to grab for it. I grabbed for it but then the guy pulled it back.

He's about two bunks from the grill. And then somebody hit me with a pipe or something, and it passed me out. I'm pretty sure it was Michael Price." From there, the lieutenant was stripped and blindfolded and continuously beaten as he was escorted to the dayroom. Lieutenant Anaya was knocked unconscious only to be revived with a bucket of water and beaten again. He heard Officer Schmitt's voice between boot-stomps, urging the lieutenant to stay awake. Schmitt was lying near him, having suffered a severe beating himself. Anaya was certain they were all going to die.

The first indications to the control center that something was amiss came from Officer Louis Cabeza de Baca, a twenty-three-year-old assigned to foot patrol. "Usually at 2:00 a.m. Roybal orders us to go inside and eat chow," de Baca told investigators. "This time I tried to get a hold of him and he didn't respond. I tried calling twice. The first time I couldn't get him, I called the control center. Officer Lucero . . . responded that everything was normal. Officer Lucero said Captain Roybal would call me back, which Roybal never did."

Peter Ray Laycock, an inmate housed across the hall from E-2 in an identical dormitory, B-2, heard the commotion and went to the door. He'd heard from an inmate in E-2 to expect something that evening. He said he saw Michael Price hit Captain Roybal across the left eye with a pipe. Soon after, Danny Macias had on an officer's uniform, unbuttoned. The inmates in E-2 emptied out into the central corridor.

According to Danny Macias, he told the crowd outside of the dorm to offer freedom to all and to make clear that participation was voluntary. In the hallway the throng split into groups, largely based on racial homogeny or, equally often, on similar goals. Macias, Michael Price, and perhaps a half dozen more inmates left, coming upon Officer Elton Curry. Curry, nearly fifty, a tall but physically awkward man the inmates called Big Foot, had just finished locking A-2, on the east side. He and Officers Juan Bustos and Victor and Herman Gallegos (unrelated) were about to open dormitory F-2 and take count when, as Elton Curry stated: "All at once, seven or eight inmates come screaming down the hallway." A guy was dressed up in an officer's uniform. Elton Curry told Juan Bustos, "Those aren't officers."

As the mob closed in on them, Officer Elton Curry radioed to Captain Roybal. Officer Curry and the other guards were horrified to hear their own message squawking from Danny Macias's hand. "There's no use calling the captain," he told them, ten feet away and grinning. "We've already got him."

Officer Curry picked up a trash can, but Danny, grinning, his crucifix tattoo winking from beneath the polyester blue shirt, stabbed Big Foot in the stomach. Curry managed to waylay an inmate named Troca before Danny stabbed him again. Michael Price pulled a fire extinguisher from the wall and struck Curry above the right eye with it. Curry dropped. Almost immediately inmates had his set of keys. While other inmates bound the officers and rushed them across the corridor to F-2, to another ersatz hostage cell (the officers were stripped, as they had been in E-2; when Officer Elton Curry's wedding ring would not come loose, inmates debated cutting off his finger—ultimately, they let him keep the ring and the finger), Michael Price took command of the radio. Officers Lawrence Lucero and Louis Cabeza de Baca, in the control center, tried to reach out for Captain Gregorio Roybal once more. This time Michael Price responded. "Listen good. We have them. We have them as hostages. You get the governor down here. You get [Corrections Secretary] Felix Rodriguez down here, and you get the press down here. You get them all down here right now, or we'll start killing motherfuckers."

Before the officers in the control center could respond, they heard an uproar and looked southward down the corridor. There they witnessed dozens of armed inmates—felons with homemade knives and clubs. Officer Lucero spotted Price with a blue handkerchief over his face and a radio in his hand. He watched Price raise the receiver; he heard Price's voice over the radio: "If you don't do what we say, this is what will happen to the fucking pigs."

Officer Lucero told investigators: "An unidentified man who was naked and had his face covered and his hands tied behind his back was brought to the front of the group of inmates. The inmate with the radio started to beat the naked man with a metal rod. Other inmates now started to beat this same man." Officer Lucero jumped on the phone to alert the higher-ups, including Deputy Warden Roberto Montoya. The inmates had Officer Juan Bustos, beating him as they went. Officer Louis Cabeza de Baca recalled, "They hit him and he finally hit the floor. They dragged him up by his hair, and he urinated himself. They were hitting him with two-foot-long pipes."

With Deputy Warden Montoya and Superintendent of Correctional Security Manuel Koroneos alerted, Officers Lucero and Cabeza de Baca followed their training: under no circumstances were they to give in to inmate demands. Once inmates realized that Juan Bustos was of no value to them, they dropped his battered body onto the cold tile. They turned their pipes on the central corridor windows. The window panels were new. Kruger and Associates had replaced the previous panes, which were waffleconed with iron bars, to three panels of large glass they claimed were bulletproof. "They may have been bulletproofed," inmate Gary Nelson joked after the riot, "but they weren't fire extinguisher–proof."

Danny Macias grabbed an extinguisher from the wall. He heaved it at the window. The windows were able to withstand the first four blows before a tiny crack emerged. Both inmates and officers fell silent for a long moment. Danny heaved the extinguisher again. More cracks. He went again, and soon thereafter the other inmates returned to the windows, their pipes falling onto the panes with even more ferocity. Officer Lucero told Louis Cabeza de Baca it was time to go. They left for the lobby of the prison. In all, Lucero estimates it took thirty seconds from the time the inmates noticed the first crack to the time at which they'd established control of the center. In their haste, the two officers left every key to the institution behind. Only twenty-two minutes had elapsed from the time Danny Ray Macias and Michael Price jumped officers in their dorm, and now inmates had control of the entire penitentiary. The first two killings happened soon thereafter.

CHAPTER SEVEN

How Jeffrey Lloyd Williams found himself inside the Penitentiary of New Mexico on that night is a fairly easy question to answer. Six months into his probation for the Debra Sibley robbery, Jeff stole a prescription pad from the pharmacy inside the Gibson's his father owned. He and a girl named Cynthia Fleury drove up to Roswell to fill the script. According to the ensuant police report:

> On April 21, 1978, Jeffrey Lloyd Williams was at Dr. John A. Most's office. He was given a prescription, but according to Dr. Most, that prescription was not for Demerol. At approximately 3:15 p.m., Paul R. Lasater, pharmacist at Palace Drug Store in Artesia, New Mexico, filled prescription order No. 36412N for 50 mg. Demerol for Terry L. Wyatt, 611 Hendricks, Roswell, New Mexico. The prescription order form was purportedly signed by Dr. John A. Most. Dr. John A. Most has told affiant that the signature on the prescription order form which he was showed is a forgery. The person who handed Mr. Paul R. Lasater the forged prescription was Jeffrey Lloyd Williams. Mr. Lasater made the identification by picking the defendant's picture out of a group of photographs of other male subjects.

Once again, the Williams family turned to Tom Cherryhomes. Cherryhomes knew his client was facing a probation violation and so a likely stint in Santa Fe. Cherryhomes delayed the trial and began to negotiate with the district attorney's office on a plea bargain. The bargain the state and Cherryhomes agreed upon would see Jeff plead guilty in exchange for a lighter sentence, one as short as seven months with good behavior.

Before his lawyer could present the deal, Jeff and two other Chaves County jail inmates rushed a guard, handcuffed him, stole his keys, and locked him in a juvenile cell. This was around 9:00 in the morning on November 5, 1978, in Roswell. While housed there and awaiting the plea bargain, Jeff talked two other inmates he shared a cell with—Ronald Patterson, an eighteen-year-old burglar, and Alton Martin, a habitual offender—into the escape plan. They hardly knew Jeff; his ability to get them to go along with the plan speaks to his manipulativeness and charm. When correctional officer Orville Freeman arrived that morning to overlook preparations for the day, Jeff met with him to complain about his access to the telephones. He said he was getting awfully tired of how the jail had been treating him. He said his civil rights had been violated. When Orville began to respond, Patterson and Martin jumped the guard.

Once they had Orville Freeman in a pair of cuffs, they forced him into a cell. The men then went to a window that had been shattered during preparation for the escape. But the pane was too narrow. Jeff, at barely 120 pounds, could not make it work. The three went back to the walkway and let Orville Freeman out of the cell. Patterson gave the jailer back his keys. In the morning, Jeff and his two accomplices were given new bonds, listed at $30,000 each.

Dubb could not post the bond. By this point, he and Roger Jenkins were back in Carlsbad, discussing the Steam Laundry arson scheme. Because the younger Williams could not make his bond and because he was deemed a risk to remain in Chaves County, Jeff was sent to the Penitentiary of New Mexico to await his trial.

He spent the rest of 1978 at Old Main. He returned to Roswell in the spring of 1979. Once back south, he and Cherryhomes met to discuss the status of his case. But whereas in the past Cherryhomes's presence had always been a comfort to Jeff, something in the young Williams had changed. The carefree and arrogant blond kid looked to have aged far beyond the 141 days he'd spent at Old Main. And rather than look for a plea bargain or a way to lighten his impending sentence, Jeff was now consumed with beating the charges altogether. He simply would not spend more time at the penitentiary. Nothing less than this would satisfy him. It was an impossibility, but one Jeff could not be swayed from abandoning. Cherryhomes's legal advice was ignored.

Though he retained his attorney, Jeff began a long campaign of pro se legal appeals, all handwritten from behind bars and all of them desperate. He filed a motion for a temporary restraining order, claiming he'd been beaten while in custody and that Chaves County Deputy Sheriff Ernie Salas remarked, "[I'd] like to blow your fucking head off." His motion was denied. Williams then claimed a member of the DA's office had made a homosexual advance on him. In response, DA Randall Walker filed a motion to have this information barred, calling it "evidence of such a highly inflammable nature that its prejudicial effects will greatly outweigh its prohibitive value." Williams's accusations were dismissed, and his motion was denied. He filed a motion to use the jailhouse telephone to contact potential witnesses on his behalf. The motion was denied. He filed a motion to use the law library. His motion was denied.

His court date was set for April 4, 1979. Desperate to derail proceedings, Jeff swallowed a razor blade on April 2. He was rushed to St. Vincent Hospital in Santa Fe. This delayed the trial by three months.

In the interim he had Cherryhomes file a petition for commitment, claiming Williams needed psychiatric treatment at the state hospital in Las Vegas and should remain there for however long his incarceration was to last. The petition was denied. Finally in July, Williams was convicted of four charges: conspiracy to escape from jail; assault upon a jailer; false imprisonment; and conspiracy to obtain a controlled substance by the use of a forged prescription. Awaiting sentencing, Williams penned the following statement to the judge:

> Comes now, the defendant in the above and entitled cause and herein petitions that this court to in the jury instructions inform the prospective jurrors [sic] that the defendant in this matter willfully asks that the penality [sic] for the offenses herein be one of the sentence of death by lethal injection as prescribed and provided for in the NMSA, 1978.
>
> The defendant in support of this herein states.
>
> 1) The penalty sought by the state's Assistant District Attorney, Ron Walker, would be a term of cinfinment [sic] to the Penitentieray [sic] of New Mexico of fifty to one hundred and fifty years.
>
> 2) The defendant is twenty-three years of age, and such a period of confinement is longer than his natural life.
>
> 3) The defendant feels that such a period of confinement is one of creul [sic] and unusual punishment in full consideration of the ridiculous nature of the matter dealt with in this cause.

The motion was denied.

On July 11, 1979, the judge ordered Jeff Williams to the PNM for a sentence of three to thirty years.

That is the timeline. Those are the facts, provided by Roswell County's oft-out-of-service microfiche for case CR-79-14. As is always true, there were other factors at play—matters even Tom Cherryhomes and Dubb Williams could not have known.

In March 1979—before Jeff swallowed the razor blade—he had added two names to his subpoena list of witnesses for the defense. His previous list had included his father, a family friend and judge named Fincher Neal, and a few Goldcoaters. His strategy to appeal to the courts as a beloved screwup with close ties to top men in society was no longer of interest to him. Now, after four months inside Old Main, he'd added the names Michael Colby and William Jack Stephens to his list of defense witnesses. Before arriving at Old Main, Jeff Williams had never heard of either man. He knew nothing about them. Back in Roswell, he had them recorded as among the closest associates in his life.

I first asked attorney Mike Stout about this. Stout's relationship with Jeff was brief. He'd represented Jeff only in the short interim between his arrest for the prescription forgery and the arrival of Tom Cherryhomes. Still, Stout knew the names Michael Colby and William Jack Stephens, and he had no idea why Jeff Williams would place them on a defense witness list. "Perhaps," Mike Stout offered, "they just wanted a ride to Chaves County."

Sue DeWalt, the first woman to graduate from the New Mexico State Police Academy, in 1976, knew nearly every high-risk classified inmate inside Old Main. "I was so tired of that penitentiary by 1980. I'd had to work two homicides and the December escape," she told me, "and whereas the inmates used to be nice to me, something had changed. They were almost openly hostile." She said her higher-ups were often too afraid to go inside the penitentiary, so they left it to DeWalt.

I asked her about Jeff. She said the name sounded familiar but that she could not recall working with him. I mentioned to her that Jeff Williams had placed Michael Colby and William Jack Stephens on his defense witness list. She paused for a moment before laughing. "Oh, god!" she exclaimed. "Are you sure of that?"

I looked back over the list of names.

"As defense witnesses!" she said. "That is about the craziest thing I've ever heard."

■ ■ ■

Michael Dennis Colby was once described in newspapers as "a gawky, homely, red-haired, freckle-faced Anglo" who "would be more comfortable in the tenth century as a Viking." Colby could "get you laughing at the most gruesome things," an inmate told the *Albuquerque Journal*. One of Colby's former attorneys, Leon Taylor, told the newspaper: "Mike's on trial for beating a man's head into a faceless pulp and he acts so at ease about the whole thing [that] he makes you feel like he's the lawyer and you're the defendant. I'm frightened of Mike."

He had the aura of a bird of prey, a vulture, with a face made more inhuman by a pair of enormous and dark aviator sunglasses. Colby had successfully argued that he had a sight condition. The specs were habitual and merely added to the intimidation, as it was never clear to other inmates or to staff exactly where Colby was looking, or why.

His father had died at age fifty-seven and had not been much of a role model. The elder Colby worked at a liquor store and had a reputation for selling booze to minors—a peccadillo that finally caught up with him in the late 1960s and caused Michael's father to lose his liquor license. The elder Colby spent his final years in a kind of Lomanesque fog, while Mildred, Michael's mother, domineered the household.

Her son had first been imprisoned around Christmas 1974, at eighteen, for armed burglary. Michael Colby had since hooked up behind bars with a tough-guy inmate and former Vietnam-era tank engineer named William Jack Stephens.

Jack Stephens was from the dusty and poor ranch town of Deming. The media described him as "handsome, blue-eyed, and interested in the Nazi party." He stood perhaps six feet tall, and whereas Colby was wiry, Stephens had a lot of bulk. He lifted weights. He kept in shape by playing handball and organizing baseball games. He had feathered hair just shy of his shoulders, which he was proud of brushing, and wore a gold ring on his right hand and earrings in his left lobe and had a muddied mess of tattoos on both forearms. Two angry cobras spit at each other from each pectoral. "The pen has anything that basically a small town would have," he told a documentary crew. "You pay bills on the street. We pay bills in here. There's no difference. It's a small society, and there are rules you got to live by. It costs. I have a laundry man that cleans my clothes and all my shit every week. I have a guy that works in the chow hall that makes special chow for me. But just like on the street: you have to pay to have extra shit. It cost me a hundred a month to live good." This is an extraordinary amount and would mark Jack Stephens as one of the wealthiest inmates within the facility. Prisoners were often paid twenty-five cents per hour—or $1.75 per week. He went on. "I gamble a bit. I have a job. I have the money. I like to walk up and down the hallway dressed real nice. I live as best I can in these conditions." His penchant for gambling earned him the nickname "Two Pack" for the cigarettes he used as chips.

By the time Colby met him, Stephens was a violent and unrepentant source of terror for the communities in which he'd lived. He was born in tiny Culwell, North Carolina, but raised more or less on the West Coast, where his father worked as an engineer. He grew up in a family of four sisters and a mother, all of whom doted on him. Jack's father left the family when the boy was twelve. The family was forced to move back to Jack's mother's hometown, Deming. After that, the sweet and handsome kid changed.

He was expelled from high school for fighting, got his GED, and volunteered for the US Army. At a time when his peers were desperate to find ways to avoid the draft, seventeen-year-old Stephens was ready to go. He joined the 32nd Armored Division, tasked with overlooking the Fulda Gap. He was dismayed to find himself in West Germany and not Vietnam. War was far off, only hypothetical here. He began drinking and, drunk, in 1968, fell off some scaffolding and broke his back.

Discharged, he returned stateside with drug and alcohol dependencies, using cocaine every so often to balance the lows. Not long after his discharge, Jack Stephens held a gun in the face of a resort manager in Washington State. He pulled the trigger, but the firing pin was misaligned. He returned to New Mexico where, high and drunk, he'd lost his mind one night over a woman and followed her and two of her passengers around in a car chase that ended only after Stephens fired a shotgun blast through the victims' windshield. Nobody was injured, but Jack found himself spending May 1977 to June 1978 inside the Luna County jail.

The attorney general's report on the riot is quick to note that prison gangs were emerging in California but had yet to infiltrate the system in New Mexico. There was one exception: a dozen or so violent Anglos had begun to adopt certain elements of the Aryan Brotherhood, a hardcore gang exploding in number inside of the California system. If it was Jack

Stephens's time in jail on the West Coast that'd introduced him to the efficacy of using gangs to control market conditions, it was while in Luna County lockup that Jack developed his own wrinkle in the trafficking vocation. In California the vast majority of contraband at the time came from visitors. Stephens immediately saw that New Mexico's system was much easier to crack. It took him no time at all to find a fault in Luna County. It came in the form of a twenty-year-old officer named Carlos Sainz Lucero, or Armando. As mentioned earlier, Lucero found himself confessing to the trafficking system he'd been involed with, claiming that in exchange for jewelry he supplied inmates in Luna County jail with drugs. The indictment also stated that Lucero had brought prostitutes and liquor into the jail, and had partied with inmates. His connection in the jail was William Jack Stephens, and Stephens was making an enormous profit.

■ ■ ■

Bert Duane Stevens (no relation to William Jack Stephens) had been picked up at age eighteen for grand theft auto and battery, in an incident that took place just east of Deming along Interstate 10. It was a first offense for the teenager, who was evaluated as having an IQ of 80. His attorney Rex Hall called him "one of the dumbest boys I believe I ever met."

It wasn't so much that Bert Stevens disliked drugs. He wasn't a reformer. The trouble was that Bert, like many behind bars at the time, had heard that the state offered informants generous compensation. For a first-time auto theft? He could expect parole in exchange for prosecutable information. And it wasn't as though taking a bad cop down was unpleasant. By late spring of 1978, Bert Stevens had uncovered the ring Jack Stephens had created. Through watching and eavesdropping, he realized that the overwhelming number of drugs he saw in the Luna County jail were too pervasive for the guards not to notice. He knew Lucero was the trafficker, and hoped to trade on this information to have his own time reduced.

Sheriff Bob Waldrop acted on the information. Soon Officer Carlos Sainz Lucero was facing years behind bars. Bert Stevens testified on the days of June 6 or 7, 1978, telling the court that William Jack Stephens was Lucero's connection behind bars. Over the course of Bert Stevens's time at Luna County, he witnessed Officer Lucero furnish for Jack Stephens and his clique ten syringes, steal prescription pills from one prisoner and give these pills to Stephens inside Stephens's cell, give marijuana to prisoners, and shoot up drugs and smoke marijuana with prisoners. He also confirmed the officer brought in prostitutes for prisoners. Stephens denied this, admitting to the court to having only received "a few drinks" from Officer Carlos Sainz Lucero because Lucero liked him.

Lucero was eventually given eleven months of jail time and placed in a special facility for his protection. As for Bert Stevens, he was transferred to the PNM to await the clearance of his plea deal.

Sheriff Waldrop and other authorities in Luna County were more than nervous about this decision. They'd tried to win support for housing Bert Stevens in the jail at home, but once this became impossible, authorities in Deming endeavored to protect their witness. County Judge Ray Hughes went so far as to visit the penitentiary and speak to Warden Clyde Malley on Bert Stevens's behalf. Malley assured both Sheriff Waldrop and Judge Hughes that Bert Stevens would be held in Cellblock Four, the prison's unit for inmates under protective custody. They were told Bert Stevens would never come face-to-face with the man he'd testified against.

This was crucial because after the conviction, William Jack Stephens now lived at Old Main as well. It was here that he met Michael Colby.

William Jack Stephens and Michael Colby were both initially housed in Cellblock Two before being switched to a maximum-security block, Cellblock Three. The pair clicked. Colby: loud, brash, with a gift for mind games. Stephens: a stoic demeanor and ferocious eyes. They learned from each other. Racketeering, intimidation, strong-arming officers in order to gain access to the personnel files of other inmates. They knew how to coerce inmates into deep debts and to pay other inmates to collect on those debts. When they ran into opposition, their tactics shifted toward gang stalking and, for the unlucky, violence.

Jack Stephens was no fan of snitches, and he didn't care if some, or even many, of those labeled were done so falsely. "We have it tough enough getting past the guards with the kind of stuff we do here," he told a documentary crew. "Once you find out somebody anywhere on the line is ratting, well. That person has to go. It's bad enough moving without the police being up on what's happening. When you have people that tell them everything? Those people have to go. Or be eliminated."

Bert had cost Jack an easy market. Now at the PNM and burned as a trafficker, Jack initially lost the scheme he'd perfected in Luna County.

Desperate, Jack turned to other measures. He was written up by Officer Tony Gutierrez, a visiting room officer. The officer wrote the following to the warden:

> At approximately 10:55 a.m. on the above date [12/21/78], I, Officer Tony Gutierrez, called in Carla Freeman from the waiting room to visit resident Stephens. When Carla Freeman approached resident Stephens at table #1, resident Stephens gave her a big tight hug and a great big and long kiss, right on the mouth. While Carla Freeman was visiting him, he moved close to her and put his legs in between hers, then he started putting his knee on her cunt and rubbing it. So then I called Officer Hoch in the front office and asked him what relation Carla Freeman was to resident Stephens and Officer Hoch stated to me that she was his stepdaughter.

This ended with a stern warning for Jack Stephens.

■ ■ ■

With his supply line cut off and a formal reprimand for incestuous behavior, Two Pack Stephens was quickly finding what little sway he held in jeopardy. Something had to be done to regain his reputation.

On April 14, 1978, Bert Stevens was led from his protective cell to the weightlifting room. He should not have been allowed into the room; he only managed to go there after he assured officers it was of his own accord. An inmate named Friese had worked as an intermediary. He'd told Bert that Two Pack Stephens wanted to reconcile. Jack Stephens and Michael Colby were already there, waiting alongside their acolyte, Michael Price. The three men had baseball bats, stolen from the baseball equipment shed and supplied to them by an unknown inmate with access to the shed. Officers were slow to respond. By the time they had, Bert Duane Stevens no longer had any bone structure to his face. He was twenty-two years old and pronounced dead on arrival at St. Vincent Hospital.

Leon Taylor served as defense attorney for Michael Colby and William Jack Stephens. It was a losing case; Taylor's clients now faced life imprisonment and potential capital punishment. Despite the high stakes—or perhaps because of them—Taylor nonetheless grilled the state's witnesses.

An inmate named Earl Austin told the court that Jack Stephens had confessed to the murder and that Michael Price had told Austin the plan was to escape from the Santa Fe jail once remanded there before the trial. But under cross-examination, Austin's own words destroyed his credibility. He'd once labeled himself a "professional snitch," and for his services he had spent his time in eight state prisons and eleven federal prisons, having to be moved constantly because of his career as an informant. Taylor also brought up Austin's mental health record and alerted judges to the fact that Austin was currently incarcerated for a threat against former president Lyndon B. Johnson's life.

Of the three other state witnesses, Taylor lambasted them, calling inmate Jim Ellis (who also claimed to have heard Jack Stephen's confession) a "sneaky embezzler." He called inmate Clyde Banks (who allegedly helped concoct an alibi for the killers) a "Judas." He claimed inmate Ronnie Fritts was the real killer, pointing to the fact that Bert Duane Stevens had once ratted on a Fritts escape attempt from Luna County; Taylor's ad hominem argument on Fritts was that he was a "perverted homosexual" and a "despicable, lewd, licentious, perverted wretch."

This made for juicy media coverage, but the evidence against Colby and Stephens—including bloodstains on Colby's pants—was overwhelming. On October 23, 1978, after less than two hours, both men were found guilty. When the defendants were offered a chance to speak on their own behalf, to show the judge their character directly, Stephens didn't say a word. Colby used his time to rail against the entire judicial system—including the court. The defendants won in this sense: Colby and Stephens were each given life sentences to run consecutively to (after the expiration of) their current terms. The actual pronouncement date would come a few months later. When leaving the courtroom, Taylor offered his best advice. He promised to work on the appeal. It didn't seem like they were listening or even cared. They were somewhere else.

In August 1979, Jack Stephens was given a parole hearing. He did not prepare for it. Why bother? A parole officer wrote to the board: "For the past ten years his life has been spent either in prison or on parole. It is felt that his involvement in the present offense is due to his distorted inmate values that dictate that an informer must be eliminated both to save one's image and pride, and to insure that prohibited activities in prison do not come to the attention of the authorities." The loss in court didn't bother him. By that point, he and Michael Colby had no intention of sticking around.

■ ■ ■

Jeff Williams's dorm at Old Main, B-1, was directly across and down one floor from E-2, where the riot began. As an appraisal, one inmate told the FBI: "B-1 is a pussy dorm. In general, they wouldn't participate." Roger Morris's assessment was that B-1 was "for the 'screw-ups,' perhaps the least popular place after Cellblock Four . . . "

B-1 housed inmates who owed other inmates a debt, who were homosexual, or who were otherwise seen as weak and easy to take advantage of.

The rioting inmates appeared outside of B-1 just as Joe Madrid, a porter who lived in the unit, was leaving E-1. Madrid had what inmates called a "kid" in E-1, and once he'd heard the uproar on the floor above, Madrid managed to pass a heavy wrench into the dorm and warn the residents to barricade themselves.

Jeff and the others inside B-1 had watched Joe Madrid pass the wrench. They took his advice and immediately went to work, turning over their bunks and stacking them against the front door to the unit. When Joe Madrid turned around to return to B-1, he saw that he'd been cut off by Michael Price and Leo Santistevan, another hardened E-2 convict. Others soon joined.

"What the fuck're you doing?" Santistevan asked him.

"It's none of your business," Joe said.

"None of my business," Leo said, and stuck Joe with a knife.

According to Peter Ray Laycock, who was watching the vestibule from the floor above, "They were striking, stabbing, stabbing, stabbing Joe Madrid." Madrid started toward B-1, his dorm, but never came close to its sanctuary. It was highly unlikely that the men inside B-1 would have taken down their ramparts in order to welcome him back inside. Jeff Williams watched from behind the safety of the grille as Michael Price took an extinguisher from the wall and struck Joe Madrid in the face. It was an ugly coup de grâce. The left side of Joe's face drooped forward, unbridled from the skull. Blood spurted across the hallway.

Over the next thirty-six hours, the reactions to violence would prove as disparate as they would bizarre. Some inmates played cards and drank coffee throughout the entire ordeal. Others tried to sleep. Later, an inmate who managed to free himself from the institution at the height of its violence wandered back inside—despite the hollered pleas from the National Guard amassed around the perimeter fencing—to raid a snack machine. The sight of Joe Madrid's murder caused some inmates in B-1 to work with an even more frenetic pace at barricading themselves inside. Many inmates froze up. This is a natural stress reaction known to clinicians as tonic immobility. Though counterintuitive, ethologists James L. Gould and Peter Arduino argue that "tonic immobility may be the best option when the animal perceives little immediate chance of escaping or winning a fight." It would make sense, then, for an inmate like Jeff, having spent his short life relying on the influence of his family, comfortable in a role where there was never a price that could not be paid, to find himself utterly without escape of fortune and thus frozen with the first real fear he'd ever felt in his life.

He had good reason to be afraid. His trek to semi-protection had begun soon after he'd been transferred from Chaves County with the escape attempt, on November 5, 1978. The next day, he found himself on the main line at the penitentiary. That same day, November 6, journalist Hadley Wells published "Anatomy of a Murder" in the *Deming Headlight*. The convictions for the murder of Bert Duane Stevens were two weeks old. Wells's piece detailed the ordeal between William Jack Stephens and Bert Duane Stevens, including the subsequent murder. The paper made the rounds inside the pen (inmates were highly conscious of how they and others inside Old Main were perceived by the media). Michael Colby and Jack Stephens had their reputations behind bars cemented. For other inmates, most far less violent but desirous of the tough-guy image, Row (short for Rojo, the Spanish term for red, indicating Colby's red hair) and Two Pack were now seen as kings of the institution.

Nonetheless, the outcome of the trial had left neither Colby nor Stephens feeling great about the culture at Old Main. As "Lil' Red" Darrell Stelly told New Mexico State Police investigators after the riot: "The thing with Mike Colby is that he just got burnt on that killing [Bert Stevens]. And he's still real paranoid about that. And he doesn't talk about the crimes at all. He hasn't given me any specifics whatsoever." It is difficult to imagine that Stephens and Colby would open up so quickly to an inmate they did not know, an inmate like Jeff Williams. It also leaves one to wonder what

Jeff was thinking, and how he managed to convince Tom Cherryhomes into signing off on the subpoenas. This was the point both attorney Mike Stout and Officer Sue DeWalt meant to relay. Colby and Stephens were only five months removed from the baseball bat murder conviction and its notoriety: Exactly what kind of character witnesses would they make?

The answer might be found in the trafficking system within the pen. According to an interview with the *New Mexican*, an inmate described how it was common for drug addicts to fall short of their debt and, in order to "make up the difference," inmates often diluted their stash with water or other liquids. The deal between the Anglo clique and Williams would be that Williams was expected to use part of his Demerol stash for himself, and to pay for it by dealing the rest. But once complaints returned to Colby and Stephens, the tone of the relationship changed. Jeff was out of money. His father could not help him. And Jeff was nothing if not two things: an arrogant and reckless young man, and a Demerol addict. It was, ultimately, what had landed him in trouble. The relationship he'd hoped to build behind bars hadn't quite worked, and now he owed dangerous men.

Further, neither Michael Colby nor William Jack Stephens had any connection to Roswell or to Chaves County. They had no reason to visit.

On the other hand, the southern county jails of New Mexico were vastly understaffed and underbudgeted, and during the 1970s they had a reputation as desirable places if you wanted access to contraband or an easier, low-pressure stint; or even where you went if you wanted to test your luck with a breakout. Las Lunas County jail recorded more than eighteen escapes between 1976 and 1978. In December 1978, it was noted in the *Roswell Daily Record* that that year alone the Roswell Correctional Center had seen eight inmates disappear. Jeff Williams was at Old Main because of his escape attempt, which meant he knew, at least on an elementary level, the weaknesses within Chaves County's facility.

Another, more alarming piece of evidence came out in interviews following the riot. According to Michael Vern Washburn, an inmate held in Cellblock Four because he'd snitched on a Chaves County escape attempt—one unrelated to Jeff Williams's—he walked through the central corridor, looking for a way to escape the institution, and passed directly by Jerry Ray James, which "kind of flipped [me] out." Washburn said James didn't recognize him, and explained their animosity. "Jerry James is the big money man in this joint. He's in big-time money and I snitched him out for . . . they were going to escape out of Chavez County [*sic*]. They had all the bars cut and everything." Almost exactly nine months before they would mastermind and execute the December escape, William Jack Stephens and Michael Colby were scheduled to appear on behalf of Jeff Williams—and therefore be housed at the compromised Chaves County jail.

■ ■ ■

By 2:30 in the morning of February 2, 1980, it became clear to the inmates inside the A&O unit that having Officer Mike Hernandez inside the dormitory with them offered no protection. In fact, he was proving himself a burden. Unlike the men in B-1, unlike his brother, Jeff, Gary and the others in intake were, by and large, too new to the prison and its rackets to have made enemies or procured debt. Some of them weren't so lucky; they'd created a bad reputation on the streets and now that they were here, it was time to answer for past disrespects. These latter inmates were terrified.

Around 3:00, some of the hardened inmates from E-2, Michael Price and Danny Macias included, appeared outside the grille to A&O. They'd spent the previous half hour searching for anything that would assist in spreading the mayhem. Beneath the prison kitchen, they found what proved to be the crucial tool for the worst of the violence: an acetylene cutting torch. By 3:15, the grille to A&O hung by a few pins and hinges, all of which were turning to a red-orange liquid. Outside, Danny Macias offered the dark morning's ultimatum. *Todos van hacer.*

An inmate, a welder, told the rest of the A&O residents he knew what the smell was. He told them, "They're coming in." Noise came in the form of laughter and chaos outside, the hissing of the torch, the dark wind howling through the broken windowpanes of the dormitory. The men in B-1 were silent.

Gary knew nobody. In fact, in ten years of searching for a concrete anecdote about Gary from his high school days, only one classmate, a woman his age, could recall anything: "On a Fourth of July, Gary let off some fireworks and one of them flew into my car through the open window. Gary jumped in and grabbed it and threw it out. It was pretty exciting! I always thought he was a nice guy."

In those quiet moments before the grille gave way, before Officer Mike Hernandez was taken hostage and the men inside the unit, here for less than twelve hours, were informally introduced to life inside Old Main, Gary fathomed, for the first time in his life, what a gift it was to be ignorable. He had struggled his entire life to be seen, to be recognized on his own merits. Harshly, ironically, that high school anonymity that had plagued and depressed him made him the envy of a different institution—one in which gossip was deadly.

Gary went back to his mattress on the floor and began to rip his bed-sheets, to form a mask. He directed a lot of other youngsters to disguise themselves. Their only option was to blend in with the angry horde. When the door finally broke free, the rioting inmates were preoccupied with Officer Mike Hernandez. Another inmate, a man from Roswell named Ray Vallejos who had been found guilty of manslaughter in a road rage incident, found himself on the wrong side of the horde. As an eyewitness named Davis told the *Albuquerque Tribune*, "There was a total of about nine persons involved in this attack. Vallejos was beaten with bars, clubs, [and] fists and was kicked several times after he was down on the floor. They called him a snitch and said he deserved to die a slow, long death."

These misfortunes gave the rest of the A&O inmates enough time to slip into the corridor and blend in among the inmates now leaving the two floors of the A and F dormitories. Only E-1 and B-1 still remained closed.

With a better view of the situation, Gary was aghast. The inmates who'd broken into the psychological wing as well as the administrative area had looked for personnel files and the notes on who had said what to which officer, under which circumstances, and how credible the information was. Once raiding convicts gleaned from them what they wanted, another crowd set all of the paperwork on fire. Their hope was to cause confusion and to argue for newer sentences or redistribution to other states' institutions. The fire quickly grew beyond containment. The corridor was thick with smoke, the gymnasium and administrative wings burning bright. The fire was astonishing, nothing like the Steam Laundry. Officer Mike Hernandez was dragged to F-1, where he was stripped and forced to join Elton Curry and the two Gallegoses in the dayroom. According to Roger Morris, once inmates had parked Hernandez in Cellblock Three, they asked him if he was a guard. "I used to be," Hernandez offered. That feeling was growing with all the personnel. By this point, Cellblock Three, home to the most hardened convicts in the state, had been opened. Inmates had rolled the acetylene torch down the corridor to Cellblock Five, the block under construction. Once they cut through the grille, they added to their arsenal another torch and an array of construction tools. Soon they appeared outside of Cellblock Three to liberate the prisoners inside. As one inmate put it, "When Cellblock Three opened, that meant death."

Oddly though, Gary felt none of this doom. To put it another way: even in severe crisis, the Williams brothers were polar opposites: Jeff fell into shock and paralysis while Gary grew clearheaded and decisive. Gary left the A&O unit to walk to Jeff's dorm, B-1, a catacorner dormitory. His brother's letters had come from the dorm, and he knew his brother beyond his antics. Jeff might've been a cocky kid, a nuisance who disrespected authority figures and allowed their father to bail him out of trouble. What Jeff wasn't was a fighter or a killer or somebody who had ever felt as though the petty crimes he committed would catch up with him. Ultimately, Jeffrey Lloyd Williams was a sort of wrestling heel or carnival barker: he could play the game a bit, and perhaps spend some time behind bars. But when something akin to a riot was happening—when there were real-world consequences—Jeff folded under the pressure.

Gary, the shy kid from Carlsbad, suddenly found resolve. He needed to find his younger brother. The destruction in the central corridor was worse than he expected. Leaving B-1, the penitentiary was in worse shape now than it had been ten minutes earlier. By the time they passed the officers' mess, the inmates couldn't see their own hands in front of their faces. Some men in the corridor were succumbing to smoke inhalation. Inmate Nick Coca was in the mess hall, his body found after the riot having died of carbon monoxide poisoning. The same fate was met by Herman Russell, a member of the Navajo Nation, and Frankie Sedillo, a burglar from Santa Fe.

But Gary managed to find Jeff's dorm and was relieved to have made it before the execution squads. Many of the inmates inside refused to leave. They felt safer staying behind. In postriot interviews, one inmate summarized this rationale: "We started calling for guards. There weren't any guards there . . . we were flashing SOSs with our lights trying to get those cops to come in and they wouldn't come in." As was true with most of the men in B-1, Jeff feared for his life. The natural bluster was gone.

Gary managed to speak some sense into his younger brother. "Keep your head down," he told Jeff and a handful of other men who finally agreed to take the agonizing walk through the corridor to the front doors of the pen.

In charge of this platoon, Gary was brave and resourceful—a surprising shift in his personality and life pattern. He didn't know it, couldn't have known it, but the riot was offering him a moment of redemption for the twenty-seven-year-old. Finally, he smelled crisp, cool air. Soon he witnessed snow rolling peacefully along the yard. The administration wing no longer had doors. In front of the group lay freedom: local and federal law authorities stood just beyond the prison's chain-link fence, urging them forward. Gary, relieved, turned to assure his younger brother. But Jeff was nowhere to be found.

PART TWO

"I get these real weird feelings, like chills, when I know something is going to happen," retired correctional officer Marcella Armijo told me. "My family says it's the Indian in us, but I don't know." Usually outspoken, there were times during our conversation whereupon Marcella became pensive. "Two nights before the riot," she said, "I was [working] in Tower Three and a fucking white owl comes and sits right there. I'm here, okay? And the owl comes and sits right next to me." She told me it was an omen. Perhaps it was. History was about to repeat itself.

In the short saga of New Mexican jurisprudence, incarceration is a recent development. The territory went more than three hundred years without anything resembling a penitentiary. The only option during early conquistador explorations was to send colonial felons on the long trek back to Compostela, a coastal garrison in western Mexico founded by the most notoriously savage of all the conquistadores, Nuno Beltrán de Guzmán. In any case, this was rare and reserved largely for friars. Noblemen who'd committed barbarous acts were punished with exility to the Philippines. As for the less fortunate, Spanish citizens often faced two hundred lashes and banishment from the New World. In his book *Men Came on Horses*, Stan Hoig writes that "any Indian even suspected of being resistant to Spanish overlording was often hanged, burned at the stake, or brutally maimed. Indian women were raped or forced into slave servitude." Most of the condemned were convicted and sentenced on the spot, with tens of thousands of Indigenous peoples being impaled, burned alive, drowned, or fed to dogs.

These were thought of as pragmatic approaches to a kingdom in Castile that was desperately bankrupt. The final defeat of the Moors on the Iberian Peninsula had cost the co-monarchy everything; it had been only after Queen Isabella I had sold her private jewelry that Spain could afford the first Columbus expedition. All succeeding conquistadores were under immense pressure to provide wealth back to their home country, and the monarchy was under immense pressure to ensure its solvency.

While the Moors had been vanquished, a new, northern form of Christianity was emerging. By the time of Francisco Vázquez de Coronado's journey into what is now New Mexico, King Francis I of France was signing the Edict of Fontainebleau as a response to anti-Catholic posters appearing on walls and signposts in the northern provinces. That Protestantism had reached France's countryside only hastened the Spanish crown's desire for financial independence and for the rebuilding of its military. Given this, thoroughly investigating and bringing through the court system a charge against a Spanish man, a Basque explorer, let's say, who has pledged his entire familial wealth for the crown and has offered to join the exploration group, for something he had done to unknown heathens in a world where, still there were steady reports of towns of gold; of gold so plentiful chieftains mixed it with milk for their nightly baths; of lagoons of liquid gold; of tribes of giants; of seven cities of gold; of a nation whose people had ears so cumbersome they dragged along the ground; of seven cities of virgins; of a tribe of people who lived on the shore of a lake and slept beneath the water at night and mountains that touched the sunshine and more than enough wealth to make Spain and the Catholic Church the only true cultures of the world—well. A criminal trial would only impede the continued efforts. And while both Coronado himself and later Don Juan Oñate, the first governor of what is now New Mexico, were remanded for lengthy and shameful trials, both men died free.

This was thanks in large part to the friars who accompanied them. The official position on imperial expansion, its raison d'être, was to spread the word of God to all mankind. *Euntes ergo docete omnes Gentes*, the Apostle Matthew implores, and this guise justified what the crown knew was to happen to the Indigenous peoples. The friars were meant to curtail any brutal actions taken by Spanish soldiers. But for both Coronado and Oñate, it was on the word of their friars that the court sided with the two explorers.

Nonetheless, brutality occurred daily. As an example, Stan Hoig writes: "Nuno Beltrán de Guzmán tortured the compliant Tangáxuan II until he revealed other caches of gold. This was still insufficient. Guzmán ordered him tied to the tail of a horse and dragged across the plains in an attempt to learn of more gold. When it was finally determined that the man had nothing left to give, he was bound to a stake and burned to death."

Many of the conquistadores returned to Spain dejected, destitute, and mocked. The fervor for endless gold was very quickly replaced with cynicism. As nobleman Marquis de Montesclaros finally described their efforts and the new people: "The light that we have thus far gathered on this expedition reveals that the people are rustic, wretched in clothes and spirit, that they do not possess silver or gold, [that they] dwell in straw and grass houses, and live on native fruits such as maize and vegetables, which they say are grown twice a year in places. Instead of cotton, I have been assured that they weave dog hair."

The explorers left behind their friars and priests, who said their desire was to continue spreading the holy faith. By some accounts, New Mexico mission towns were soon inhabited by 80 percent illicit offspring of these holymen.

Even after the territory managed to disencumber itself from its colonial potentates and psychotic friars, carceral matters were not prioritized. If a crime was committed, it was best to decide if the perpetrator deserved to pay a fine or to hang from the gallows. Those deemed necessary for serious confinement were transported to Leavenworth, while the few who remained were housed in laughable institutions. Reports mention cells constructed only of rotting timber. One account, from 1853 in Doña Ana County, describes a cell door held together with twine. The convicted were jailed, only to escape. These escapes were often met with relief by administrators: it was easier to run a prison without inmates. As way of example, in 1852 Santa Fe sheriff R. M. Stevens wrote to the governor to say he had no means by which to feed the fourteen inmates under his custody. They were starving, the sheriff claimed. In response, Governor James S. Calhoun simply pardoned all parties.

In 1885 the territory's legislature granted $150,000 for the construction of the Santa Fe jail. Once the building was completed at the corner of Cordova Road and St. Francis Drive, socialites danced the night away in the jail's main yard—men in tuxedos, women in bright gowns—celebrating New Mexico's first public building. As reported by the *New Mexican*: "From 8 to 10 o'clock the crowd poured into that magnificent structure until every chair in the building was held at a premium and the grand chapel hall was filled with gay promenaders."

But life inside the first jail was no dance. Quickly, the passive attitude of prior years was replaced with harsh discipline. Insolence was met with beatings and months in shackles. Brick kilns were added. Men, chained together, spent seven days a week working the brickhouse. Three months after its opening, a lifer walked up to the fourth tier and tossed himself over the railing. Death was preferable. "You think you want to know the weight of hell," one correctional officer told a reporter for the *Santa Fe New Mexican*, "talk to them guys. They know it well enough."

Sixty years after its construction, the jail had become a carbuncle in the otherwise beatific town. The walls of the jail were crumbling, and concrete and bricks often rained down, hospitalizing vendors and pedestrians along

Cordova. New Mexico's first, official foray into what the rest of the United States deemed respectable had been a disaster.

Still, it would take until an uprising in 1953 to shut down the jail for good. That year, a small man with scoliosis led a violent uprising. His name was Homer Lee Gossett. From Arkansas, Gossett had nearly two decades of jailbreaks on his record before finding himself out west. Gossett's first escape occurred at age thirteen, from a boy's school in Topeka, Kansas. In his twenties, he escaped a chain gang in Tennessee. He escaped the jail in Hammond, Indiana. He escaped the jail in Jefferson City, Missouri, and a Shelby County, Missouri, institution before spending a year on the lam, stealing cars along Route 66 and landing, finally, in northern New Mexico. After a botched attempted robbery on the Handmaids of the Precious Blood convent in Jemez Springs, Gossett turned himself in. Homer Lee told the press, "I came to the conclusion that I couldn't keep living that kind of life. If I went on the way I was going, I'd either have to kill somebody or be killed myself. And I don't want no rap like that."

His repentance lasted fourteen months.

On a June night in 1952, Gossett and an accomplice stabbed a guard to death with a pair of shears, hoping once again to abscond. This was the first noted incident in New Mexico in which a prison guard was murdered by inmates. The *Albuquerque Journal* placed blame squarely on the conditions at the facility. Writing for the *Albuquerque Journal* the day after the incident, Mel Mencher concluded:

> The slaying of a prison guard at New Mexico's ramshackle state penitentiary has again focused attention on conditions behind the crumbling dirty-red brick walls that blight the landscape south of Santa Fe.
>
> There is much more to be told about the prison than the story of a bad physical plant leading to overcrowded conditions, which is the usual rationalization of prison authorities. . . . Had the prison authorities been tougher with the known bad actors behind bars the prison guard who was killed this week might still be alive. The two men accused . . . were known to be dangerous. Their records make it clear that they not only had attempted to escape before but that they were tough guys.

The trial was a sensational one, covered by every major newspaper in the region. Gossett's notoriety spiked following a guilty verdict. He reveled in it. Journalists stood outside the redbrick jail as Gossett was led inside. Homer Lee grinned for photographers. He shouted, "This hick prison can't hold me!" and promised another breakout.

Even while in solitary, Homer Lee was forced to wear an eighteen-pound iron ball shackled to his ankle. He was thirty-four years old. In mid-June 1953, the rest of the nation was moving at light speed toward the future. That same week in Washington, DC, more than thirteen thousand people had gathered to demonstrate outside the White House, urging clemency on behalf of Julius and Ethel Rosenberg. The couple were scheduled for execution. The country was racing headlong into the nuclear age—thanks in no small part to the experiments conducted in Los Alamos. Only in Santa Fe, nowhere else in the free world, was the ball and chain still considered appropriate.

By the time Gossett was behind bars in Santa Fe, the prison staff no longer cared about such matters as humane treatment; they wanted only to maintain what little control they still had. Three wardens were hired and fired in two years. In a desperate attempt for order, the state promoted Ralph Tahash to deputy warden. Tahash, a fifty-one-year-old who'd previously served as a training officer for guards, cracked down on the institution.

The particulars of the June 1953 riot remain unclear—though what is known about the incident eerily parallels the 1980 riot. Early that morning a guard opened the cells to two convicts for a sweep. Soon, chaos broke out, and prisoners armed with knives took all twelve guards on duty hostage. At some point Homer Lee was freed from his cell. Gossett became the lead inmate negotiator, forcing Tahash into the back of the hospital and speaking to the outside world through him. Demands were straightforward: prisoners wanted Tahash to resign. They gave Tahash a 1:00 p.m. deadline.

Over the course of the next seven hours, administrators later told the press, loose convicts settled scores and raided the hospital for drugs. Dan H. Carter, head nurse for the jail, told the *Albuquerque Journal* that inmates "got small quantities of phenol-barbital plus nearly 20 CCs of Demerol." As the drugs took over, Tahash later stated, the inmates were "getting pretty fanatic."

Around 2:00 that afternoon, an hour past the deadline, Homer Lee Gossett became agitated and grabbed a tear gas canister. The canister went off in his hands. Gossett dropped it. In the ensuing confusion, Ralph Tahash broke a hospital window with his elbow. A guard outside handed him a .30-30 carbine. Tahash shot Gossett in the neck and another inmate in the stomach. Homer Lee bled to death. The riot ended soon after.

The next morning's *Albuquerque Journal* front page read: "Two Killed in State Pen Riot." Ralph Tahash appears just below in a Panama hat and tie, his sleeves rolled, a broad grin on his face. The journalists played to his tough-guy persona. "Tahash shot Gossett and Benavides as the police ran into the hospital shooting in the air. The prisoners, their leaders dead . . . scream[ed] for mercy, as they hid under beds and threw themselves on the floor crying."

In a separate article, Ralph Tahash is given room to expound on his own heroics: "Speaking with difficulty because of the heavy dose of tear gas, which he received in the closing moments of the uprising, Tahash said, 'I certainly plan to return behind the walls tomorrow morning.' He said that today's action by police and guards 'should teach them we're not fooling.'" For his efforts, Ralph Tahash was given the warden position at Alcatraz in 1961.

But Tahash was the only winner. The citizenry were outraged and embarrassed. On June 16, 1953, the *New Mexican* ran "New Pen—Now!" on its front page. The editorial begins:

> Monday's riot could not have happened in a modern penitentiary. . . .
> Modern penitentiaries have remote controls for locks, have double
> and triple precautions against seizure of guards and keys carried by
> guards. In all but archaic prisons like ours trouble in one section can
> be isolated and snuffed out quickly, before it spreads. . . . Human
> beings will not live peaceably, for long, in dirt and degradation. Filth,
> cockroaches, foul air, crushing monotony and depravity are the lot of
> penitentiary inmates in New Mexico. We must have a new peni-
> tentiary, and we must have it as quickly as mortar can be applied to
> stone.

The public agreed.

To design the new institution, the prison board chose W. C. Kruger & Associates. Willard Kruger was, without question, the most respected architect in New Mexico—and perhaps the entire Southwest. He had designed the New Mexico State Capitol building, the old Governor's Mansion, and the secret Project Y, at Los Alamos during the Manhattan Project. Kruger asked for $7 million. The prison board had only $4.5 million at its disposal but the state legislature acted quickly and soon found the additional funds. They did not barter with Kruger; they paid him in full. The decision was lauded by the public. The embarrassment of the old jailhouse would be replaced with nothing short of the best: The new pen promised to be a public works facility the rest of the world would admire and envy. A touring journalist flaunted the institution's safety protocols:

> Four of the two-story, glass domed guard towers with the fence "indented" so that the guard can command both the inside of the inner 10-foot chain link fence and the chalk-paved space between it and the other 12-foot barrier. The only openings in the fence will be the pedestrian entrance building and the vehicle sally port. At both gaps sliding gates are arranged with electrical interlocks, making it impossible to open both the inside and the outside gates at the same time.

Once a visitor had cleared the fences and the towers, they went through a Space Age safety check. "After visitors register at the information desk in the entrance building, they will be required to step on a platform where an employee will make the 'x-ray' check for weapons. If suspicious shadows appear on the Inspectoscope screen, a guard will make a further check."

The Inspectoscope was a precursor to the machines currently used by the TSA. Developed in the early 1950s largely to combat diamond smuggling, the machine cost $8,000, sat eight feet long and seven feet high, and, according to the *New Yorker*, "weighed as much as an elephant . . . and consists of a low platform with a cabinet full of unspeakably complicated electrical equipment." It was said that the safety measures at PNM eclipsed the prison in Tracy, California, which was considered at the time to be the pinnacle of prison planning. The *Clovis News-Journal* declared the new pen an "asset to the state."

"The floors, walls, railings, windows, and all surfaces of wood, metal or masonry gleam with cleanliness and polish," wrote a reporter for the *Carlsbad Current-Argus*. A decade after it had opened, Warden Harold A. Cox had a fetish-like desire to keep the place clean. Cox wanted to avoid an "institutional smell" and did so by foregoing disinfectants. He told a visiting judge the prison was kept clean via "soap and elbow grease." No posters were allowed on the walls. There was no dust and no insects. Sanitation and pride were what mattered. Cleanliness is next to godliness.

Speaking of the divine, if you were to move south from the central office you would find the two chapels—one Protestant, one Catholic. The overwhelming majority of prisoners were Catholic, though there were a few Armenian Apostolics, members of the Native American Church or other various Indigenous religions, and, of course, men who'd altogether lost interest in a higher calling.

In those early days, the men ranged from eighteen to seventy-one years of age, less than half of them still were married, most of them were divorced, and most of them were locals. Texans accounted for 15 percent of the population. There were four native Mexicans, one inmate from Canada and one from Denmark, and all of them, a decade after the prison doors had opened, were kept well-fed and busy: "With the exception of 25 to thirty men at a given time" a journalist reported, "all of the prison population is employed, and one-fourth of the population is learning, either in school or in a trade class, or both." There was the commercial print shop, the largest in the state; the brickyard; and a shoe shop where prisoners learned leathercraft and cobbling while repairing inmates' boots. Barbering was taught in the large and state-of-the-art barbershop. The bakery, with its enormous facility, allowed men interested in complex baking to train every day: indeed, in the main corridor it was a morning commonality to smell fluffy rolls. There was a TV, typewriter, and radio repair shop; a tailor; a cabinetmaking shop. The pen had a welding shop. The medical facilities within the prison rivaled those at St. Vincent, Santa Fe's hospital. The PNM had an operating room, a pharmacy, psychological services round-the-clock, and a disease treatment facility.

In the 1880s, when Santa Fe was granted the first territorial-wide correctional facility, Albuquerque had been granted the flagship university. A half century of derision and embarrassment looked to be coming to an end. Santa Fe could now compete with its much larger sibling.

■ ■ ■

I'd known Marcella Armijo's name long before we spent time together at Armijo's mobile home on the northeast side of Albuquerque. Today, a quarter of correctional officers are female. In 1976, the year Marcella joined the staff at Old Main, she was the first and only woman working in an all-men's prison. The facility she walked into on her first day had nothing in common with the one Kruger had devised.

She did not have to be there. While many guards were high school dropouts, Marcella was the middle of three daughters born into an accomplished family. Her older sister later became the New Mexico secretary of state, while her niece serves as artistic director for Teatro Nuevo Mexico in the National Hispanic Cultural Center. Marcella never felt comfortable attending the winter ball at the opera house. She was far more comfortable in the bars around the Railyard District. There, she drank, smoked, cursed, and, finally, adopted tattoos. Marcella never fit the stereotype of the overlooked middle child—to say nothing of the demure Chicana.

By the mid-1970s, Marcella's parents had had enough of her listlessness. Her father was running for a seat on the city council, and he demanded his daughter find employment. She applied to work at the penitentiary. She was twenty-five years old. Corrections did not know what to do with her. To say the least, it was not the career trajectory her parents had wished for her. Which is why she'd chosen it. *You want me to get a job? Here's a job.*

"On the first day, they told me not to get *involved* with the inmates," Marcella said. "They were looking at me, the only female. 'Don't get *involved* with the male inmates.'" She rolled her eyes.

If it'd been sheer insouciance that'd led to her application, it was the day-to-day fundamentals of the work that kept her there. She was good at her job, and she liked it. "As the only female in the prison," she told me, "they gave me a lot of shit. Not just the inmates. The other guards, too. But I gave it right back. They learned pretty soon I was tough. I was tough, but fair. That's what inmates respected." It became evident to all that Armijo was a legitimate officer early into her tenure. Only six weeks into her job, Armijo made headlines for capturing an escaped convict while off duty. The story is remarkable: Marcella and her husband lived in a trailer not far from the prison. After work one evening, a neighbor asked if there had been trouble at the penitentiary. Marcella mentioned the escape. Her neighbor told her he had seen some men dressed oddly prowling their mobile home park. As the *Albuquerque Journal* reported:

She and a friend borrowed a pair of binoculars, with one functional lens, and began scanning the horizon for suspicious movement. . . . By chance, at about 4 p.m., she spotted a man limping about. When a [State Police helicopter] came nearby, she noticed, the man ducked behind a bush. At her insistence, she and her husband drove out to the man in their pickup truck.

She recognized the clothing on him as that worn by prison inmates. Unarmed, Mrs. Armijo got out of the truck, put the escapee's hands behind his back and held him there while her husband drove off to tell a neighbor to call State Police. . . . State Police were led to where Marcella Armijo was holding Jacob Armijo [no relation] who has been serving a lengthy sentence for heroin trafficking.

The news article's headline touts "Matron at Penitentiary Displays Her Initiative" and describes her as "a woman with self-assurance, pluck, and initiative."

Armijo recalled the headline with disdain. "Plucky?" She laughed. "I was doing my fucking job."

This is not to say Armijo's life inside Old Main was without trouble. There were certainly inmates and fellow COs who saw her gender as a weakness. She described an incident during chow when she broke up a fight only to find herself in the middle of one for her own life. After the initial fight had been quelled, Armijo said, "I looked down the corridor and here comes this asshole with a big old shank. He started stabbing at me. Kicking and punching me everywhere. I don't know how I did it, but I got a good hit right in the balls. He dropped the shank. It happened so fast I didn't even know what I'd done 'til one of the inmates told me: I picked up the shank and said, 'Come at me now, motherfucker!' The hall was lined with inmates; they wanted me to know that they weren't going to get involved. All they did was stand back."

I asked her what the outcome was.

"I was fine until I kind of relaxed. I went into the captain's office to do the report. Fuck, I couldn't hardly move my right shoulder. I had torn muscles in my back. They said I could stay out of work for two weeks. I said, 'No way.' I went back to work the following day. As I was going up the ramp the warden met me and said, 'You know, Marcella, you don't have to come in today.' But if I wouldn't have gone back that afternoon the inmates would've thought I was scared or weak. I couldn't let that happen."

Officer Armijo rose through the ranks. Her personal life thrived as well. Armijo and her husband had a daughter. Her life was on a strong trajectory. In her own way, she was cutting a path on par with her successful sisters. She was respected by both inmates and officers early into her tenure. Part of what the inmates appreciated with Armijo was that she understood how their lives worked. "You don't rat when you're inside. When an inmate told me something, I never divulged that information." She recalled the relationship she had with William Jack "Two Pack" Stephens. Rumors had spread that Stephens and some of his Anglo clique had come across hacksaw blades carelessly left behind by a construction crew. "When I heard that, I called Jack over to me. I said, 'Jack, I'm about to make rounds. If you bring the hacksaws to me and slide them under the captain's door, I won't tear down your house. No questions asked. If not, you know what's coming.'"

"And he did it?" I asked.

"He did it. Nobody knew it was him. He brought them to me. That's the kind of relationship we had. He knew he could trust me not to rat him out."

Speaking generally, Marcella said, "Most of the prisoners were scared shitless. Most of them were drug addicts or thieves, shoplifters. They have no idea what to expect in prison. We had to lie to them, tell them to do their number and keep to themselves. Knowing there's no fucking way to do that."

Armijo found herself working in a dysfunctional institution. In Attorney General Jeff Bingaman's 150-page report, the term *nepotism* is used only once—"9:25 a.m. Inmate complains of nepotism at penitentiary"—but it appears in nearly every book or article previously written about New Mexico corrections during that era.

Roger Morris does an excellent job listing the bonds Deputy Secretary Felix Rodriguez shared with those who would later ascend to the highest ranks within the department. From *The Devil's Butcher Shop*:

They included the security chief, [Manuel] Koroneos, one time roofer and truck driver, a high-school dropout with no previous corrections experience who applied to the pen in 1962. . . . He was duly promoted to Lieutenant, cited for his vigilance in watching the visitors' room, and eventually made Superintendent of Correctional Security. Before Koroneos had come Eugene Long, another local high-school dropout who tried taxidermy, drove heavy equipment, and worked briefly in an army disciplinary barracks before joining the old brick house prison as a guard at the same year Rodriguez was hired. Later . . . Long rose through Captain, Assistant Warden, and Superintendent of the women's prison as well as Chief of Penitentiary Security.

These bonds were familiar, but Morris points out that they were familial, as well:

At the time of the riot, Rodriguez's brother-in-law, once a prison security officer, was head of prison industries. Eugene Long was married to Rodriguez's cousin, who once taught cosmetology classes at the pen. One captain had a brother on the prison infirmary staff; another supervised two sons as junior guards. [Adelaido, another officer with Felix Rodriguez since 1956.] Martinez's nephew worked in prison administration, while the penitentiary staff included two pairs of husband-and-wife guards, a father and two sons who were correctional officers, [and] three more officials in various offices who are all from the same family.

Felix Rodriguez's patriarchy also served to undermine the authority of any reformer, outsider, or new warden. A prisoner described this sentiment to the State Police task force: "[Warden Harold Griffin] is a puppet. Because Montoya, Korneos, Chilly Willie Martinez (a notorious snitch), and Green Eyes (a barbaric lieutenant who regularly beat inmates) . . . all of them are the ones that run this place. Griffin didn't run nothing." These men were Rodriguez acolytes.

As frustrated wardens left the state after brief, failed stints at reform and progress, it was Felix Rodriguez who was called, again and again, to save the prison—acting as not only warden in his own right but also as deputy warden twice before finally landing in the secretary position. He was Mister Fix-It, and this is likely why inmates respected him. He listened, and during times of chaos, his hand might've been cruel but at least it was steady.

This quagmire meant the prison was always in a state of flux; that outside reformers with no close ties to the institution or the state were immediately distrusted by an inner group; and that the nepotism involved in the department led to chaotic stewardships of the prison, which were quelled only when the reformers left and Rodriguez was allowed back at the helm.

Rodriguez, who had become a guard at the old jail in 1954 and who otherwise had no training in corrections—theoretically, or otherwise—had grown to rely heavily on what was called the snitch jacket. By far the largest contributing factor to the atmosphere of paranoia inside PNM was that of the "snitch jacket game." This "game" was the cruelest, most-cited tool coercion officers had at their disposal—one they relied on with increasing frequency when they felt their grip loosening from control of the prison.

The jacket worked thusly: if an inmate refused to inform, an officer would simply tell the inmate's housing unit that the inmate had indeed informed; equally often, if an officer simply disliked an inmate, that officer would spread rumors throughout the cellblock that the inmate was a snitch, thus hanging a jacket on him. On a daily basis prisoners had to navigate this hellacious game. Officers knew the code of inmates, and it left those threatened with a jacket to either prove themselves to be "on the regular" by way of violence—and therefore longer sentences—or to comply with staff and "PC-up." But agreeing to protection almost always proved to be of no value to an inmate. After the riot, Michael Colby explained the general feeling about Cellblock Four inmates, held by both general population prisoners and the staff. "Who gives a fuck about them? They were in a six-by-nine living two or three of 'em like that. Once they [police] got the usefulness of them testifying or giving up the information, they were useless to [administration]. Matter of fact, they were a burden to [administration] because [administration] had to take care of [informants]. So, no. They didn't give a fuck about that. At all."

The names of the snitches, if not made available publicly, were given to inmates in absurdly bizarre and obvious ways. In an anonymous interview with the attorney general's task force, one inmate described the maddening absurdity:

They want to get out and the only way out is snitching. So they go through the channels. Inmates write requests to [the warden]. The warden then locks them up in protection. But I know he let their names be public on purpose because he left a list of informants in his laundry. We do all of their laundry—their shoes and all of that. He's got these snitches he's going to protect, right? What he did is he put their names on a list and put it in his jacket and sent his suit to laundry. They found it in the laundry. And the informant is out there in population acting cool. Like, what's up, man? What's happening, bro? You know. Playing the good part. But they found a request with his name and number.

The task force was offered more than one glimpse into the game:

Q: Do you think the warden purposefully burned snitches, or?

A: Yeah. They use them.

Q: Once they've used them, they don't care what happens?

A: They don't care. They use them. Oh, they promise them parole. They promise them everything. But when it comes down to it, when you get out on the line? "I don't even know you, man." Rata, you know. They call him rata. And that inmate stays in his jacket. And it stays on him, even if he's transferred to a different institution. That jacket travels with him.

Q: Word gets around.

A: From that day forward. From the day he started snitching, he's no good. He can't live with that jacket, man.

Another inmate discussed the bluntness, the publicness the officers used in this game. He told attorney general investigators, "I wasn't in there a week when a captain called me to his office to ask me what was going on in the dormitory. He told me I had a lot of time to do and that if I was smart I would do it the right way—as an informant. I told him I didn't know what he was talking about. He started screaming at me and called me white trash." The next day the inmate was ordered to report for an examination "on suspicion [of] homosexual activity." The inmate said these tests were never administered, but their occurrence remained on his record:

A: I came in here with a jacket on me. When I got up here, the guy I was involved with put one on me. He and I have all kinds of friends here. So when I got up here, I would be in the mess hall and they would all be pointing at me, you know. A big group of dudes would just be pointing at me, looking at me, talking about me and stuff. I used to hate that. I'd tell them, "You got anything

to say you come tell me. Don't be talking like a bunch of women."
They have it out for me. I've got a lot of friends, but there's a lot of
guys who won't associate with me.

Q: So did you ever get rid of the jacket?
A: Can't get rid of it.

Marcella hated the jacket system, but she saw nearly every one of her
colleagues as well as her higher-ups using it. Even as she was respected by
inmates for not ratting, the stress was becoming too much for her. As was
the case with Sue DeWalt, she found inmates who were typically friendly
turning hostile toward her.

Aside from the general unease, there was also more concrete evidence
to point to: on January 11, prison psychologist Marc Orner, who was not
quiet about the intelligence he was receiving from inmates, wrote a memo
to upper administration. Its tone was beyond urgent. Twenty days before
the riot, the psychologist told his bosses that inmates were planning to
take hostages using homemade zip guns currently cached in dorm E-2.
It was Orner to whom inmates began confiding when an escape attempt
was looming in December 1979. Orner had warned the administration
then, and they did nothing. Orner says his memo produced a list of twelve
shot callers—prisoners with enough pull to influence the entire inmate
population. The list included the names of Michael Colby, William Jack
Stephens, and Mike Price. A shakedown found no evidence. The warden
thanked him. The tone was flippant, and Orner, a Philadelphian, told
them: "I'm not going to be in this fucking place when shit goes down."
After that, he refused to work on weekends.

On January 23, Deputy Warden Robert Montoya wrote a similar report
to Warden Gerald Griffin, and again a shakedown was conducted. Again, it
failed to turn up anything. Finally, on January 31, 1980, Officer Larry Flood,
who had been placed in charge of intelligence sharing, held a meeting
that included Deputy Secretary Felix Rodriguez, Warden Gerald Griffin,
and Deputy Warden Robert Montoya, along with nine other top-ranking
officials. No system-wide plan was agreed upon; the reaction by officers
to this intelligence ultimately remained with the captain on duty at any
given time. Some captains requested their officers use more care and
caution while working. Other captains failed to educate their staff at all
to the concerns.

Captain Gregorio Roybal's night shift for February 1–2 included Officer Marcella Armijo. She was supposed to be on duty, working at the control center, but around 7:00 that evening a friend had called her. It was her friend's birthday.

"She said, 'Come on, Marcella.' I said, 'Oh, no. I gotta work tonight.' She said, 'Well, just come with us and have dinner.' I said, 'Okay.'" Marcella laughed. "The tension at work had been terrible, so I had a drink. Then I had another. Then another." Marcella did not make it to her shift. She opted to stay at the smoke-filled Estrada Room, connected to Coronado Lanes Bowling, dancing and drinking until midnight. Though she told me the stress at work was a compelling factor in her missing her shift, she was adamant that it was not because of rumors of the riot. For one, rumors of a riot had become almost so common that many were ignoring their plausibility. Marcella said she also felt an obligation to be with the rest of the staff. Instead, drunk, Marcella drove to her mother's house and fell asleep. She told me she dreamt again of the white owl. It opened its beak to tell her something. She never made out what it meant to convey.

■ ■ ■

In the daylight hours Archie Martinez was a five-foot-four, 140-pound, pudgy-faced but handsome kid with a full head of black hair he slicked back with Brylcreem. At night, however, the townspeople of the tiny mountain town of Chimayó swore he transformed into a wild dog. Beneath skies overpopulated with stars and a burning moon, young Archie let himself inside the houses of his neighbors and stole whatever he fancied. His ability to burglar and disappear is what led to the mythos. When he was finally arrested and sent to the Santa Fe jail, he shimmied through the bars. Caught, he was given five years at the Penitentiary of New Mexico. There, his identity changed. At Old Main, he was not known as a wild dog but as "King of the Rats."

For this he had been housed in the protection unit, but a recent conduct violation found Archie in the hole—housed in the basement of Cellblock Three, the most dangerous cellblock in the institution. His neighbors included Bobby "Barbershop" Garcia, William Jack "Two Pack" Stephens, and Michael Colby.

After the rioting horde had taken over the institution, some inmates went to Cellblock Three to release their pals. Michael Price released inmate Darrell Jean Stelly. The two men then released Michael Colby and William Jack Stephens from the basement. The basement cells had additional security measures, and as they struggled through them, Darrell Stelly told investigators he witnessed the attack on Archie:

> A group of Chicanos came down, about six of them. And they went to cell 67 and they were standing out in front of it. I went up and asked him, "What's happening?" And he told me, "We got to kill this son-of-a-bitch, man. That's Primi Martinez. We got to kill him." I said, "Now come on, be cool." And he told me, "No, no man. We got to kill him. He's a snitch." I told him, "No, man." 'Cause by, at this time I was getting a lot of static over the radio from, from [Deputy Warden] Montoya. And Mr. Montoya was telling everybody to stay cool, and that we'd negotiate. And I told them, "Don't, don't start nothing, man. 'Cause we're trying to negotiate." And he told me, he says, uh, "No, fuck it. We're going to kill him." They had him in the corner and they were beating him and beating him and beating him. And he was screaming and screaming and screaming. . . . I stepped in the cell, and I said, "Archie," or, uh, I called him Primi . . . I said, "Primi, are you all right?" And he sat up and he says, "Little Red, you know I didn't hurt nobody, man. I didn't snitch on nobody, man. I didn't snitch on nobody, man. You know that."
>
> They went back into the cell and started beating Archie Martinez some more. The door was still open . . . and Archie looked up and he saw them coming back in the cell and he started yelling, "Please, Little Red, help me; Little Red, help me. You know I didn't snitch on nobody, Little Red. Help me." And I just turned around and I walked away.

According to the attorney general's report, Archie Martinez's death occurred around 3:00 in the morning on February 2. Around this same time, Joe Madrid was killed between dorms B-1 and E-1, and within the same half hour, a twenty-four-year-old inmate from Las Cruces, Lawrence Cardon, a car thief, never managed to leave Cellblock Three. He was stabbed dozens of times in the chest and neck through the cell bars and bled to death on the floor. There is little information on who wanted him killed or why. Thus these early killings of Joe Madrid, Archie Martinez, and Lawrence Cardon were brutal in their rage and in their techniques. They were isolated incidents, happening in different units and at the hands of different assailants. They were, frankly, the sort of violence you would expect from a prison controlled by its inmates. Not until the raid on the prison pharmacy did the violence take on a sense of the extraordinary.

For some inmates, control of the institution meant settling scores. For many others, it meant the first access to serious narcotics since conviction. Inside, prisoners found the Dalmane, the antipsychotic Triavil, the muscle relaxant Parafon Forte, injectable Valium, phenobarbital, Demerol, and any number of pain medications and anxiolytics. Experts later claimed, accurately, that these drugs were likely not the cause of violence; rather, they led to a tremendous number of overdoses. "Everybody who was up was getting down," Michael Colby later said of the pharmacy. It was not until the inmates found copier fluids, liquid paper, and other inhalants from the mechanical shop that psychosis set in. Specifically, inmates found gallons of A. B. Dick copier fluid held in tin cans. Toluene poisoning is known to cause hallucinations and irritability. Whereas the first thirty minutes or hour of the riot were frenzied and sometimes brutal, they were, more or less, conducted with the air of a mad party. The officers were quelled; the dormitories were opened; the drugs were free-flowing. The only low point in their campaign was that inmates operating under a rumor that the command center held a cache of rifles and handguns proved to be untrue. Prisoners found only tear gas canisters and two launchers, gas masks, shields, batons, and helmets.

On the wall outside of the pharmacy, an inmate—the name long since lost to history—had painted an enormous portrait of Ha'al-lk'-Mam-Chak-Ek', a Mayan god whose name translates, roughly, to the Dark Grandfather of Rain. One of several gods associated with Venus and found within the Dresden Codex, the oldest book written in the New World, the Dark Grandfather looks over the first of five 584-day cycles. He defends himself with a shield while preparing to toss a javelin at the heart of the earth. His eyes are wide. His smile is void of reason. He warns that the cycle will begin with great pestilence and starvation. Drought. Destruction. His appearance in the morning sky is a warning—not of avoiding warfare but of beginning it. When it rises in the east as the morning star, it brings with it the chaos of the underworld and a desire for human blood.

■ ■ ■

By all eyewitness accounts, the death squads that formed in the pharmacy were multiethnic, with a large percentage of the group Chicano. Michael Colby and William Jack Stephens led a small but tight group of Aryans that included Darrell Stelly and Michael Price, the bikers from E-2, and, later, some men who were loathed by other Anglos but wanted to prove their merit. This included inmates Richard Buzbee and Mike French, whose attempts to impress Colby and Stephens led to two of the most brutal homicides within the prison. A Black inmate named Reggie Bell was also pointed out as a leading member of a third squad. Peter Laycock summarized this protean relationship: "The Chicanos had taken over. But the white guys were the ones that were speaking. The Chicanos would stand back and let them speak." By *speaking*, Laycock means giving orders during the riot. In any case, the death squads operated for different reasons and for different causes, but all had one location in mind.

Cellblock Four was the farthest north designated block. The three-tiered unit had windows facing both the north and the south. Inmates housed on the north side could see beyond the prison to the Madrid Highway. Inmates housed on the south side had a view of seventy-five yards of empty dirt yard followed by the north side of Cellblock Three—an identical block, so that north-facing Three and south-facing Four could see into each other's units.

James Bunch, the A&O inmate who authorities had decided to send to Four rather than Gary Williams, was escorted to where he would spend the night with a porter named John Burrell. Their cell, 61, was on the middle tier, facing south, toward Cellblock Three. Burrell and Bunch, like many protected inmates in the block, spent the evening listening to the radio or watching television (another point of animosity, as only Cellblock Four and Cellblock One, the honors unit, were allowed their own televisions within cells).

There were other men spending their first night or their first few nights on what was sometimes referred to as the "red line block." Charlie Johnson had been moved to cell 16 from the honors dorm, A-2, for refusing to take medication. "I told the captain I did not want to go to protection," Johnson said. "He told me I was going. So I told an officer about the riot [that] was gettin' ready to come down, that they had been passing a note around. The words that he said was, 'Bullshit.'"

That night, David Fuentes and his cellmate, Kari Orensen, spent the evening in their normal routine. Their cell was on the north side, facing away from the rest of the institution. Fuentes told State Police, "We played cards early that evening, and [Kari] wrote a letter and I wrote a letter. Then we went to sleep."

Another inmate, David Peterson, housed in cell 89 on the south side of the unit, began his night routinely as well. "On Friday, February 1, I received a visit from my mother. After the visit I came back to the cell and went to sleep. About 2:30 or 2:00 in the morning I heard commotion. I heard people talking in the cellblock saying they're breaking out of Cellblock Three. I didn't believe it at first. I got up and looked over to Three. At first I didn't see anything. And then somebody said, 'There's the acetylene torch,' and then I knew it was for real."

Cellblock Four inmate Melvin Thomas remembered: "We heard commotion on the other side of Four. People hollering, like, a lot of conversations. . . . [James] Weaver hollered through the vent to me and said, 'They're having a riot. It's kicking off.' We couldn't see Cellblock Three from where we were. The guys were telling us they had a cutting torch and were running back and forth and they had hostages, and they were leading them around blindfolded, without their clothes on."

Any inmates who had assumed officers would help Cellblock Four were soon dismayed. An anonymous inmate told the attorney general's task force: "The guard in my cellblock left around 1:30 or 2:00. He went out the front door and never came back. The reason I know this is because the phone rang at about 2:15; it was evidentially from the front. The phone was never answered. It just kept on ringing."

When asked to elaborate, the inmate stated, "You could hear him going down the hallway. You could hear his keys rattling. You heard nothing after a while. Then someone hollers, 'There goes our guard.'"

David Fuentes told investigators what happened next. "Jim Gossens said there was a riot going on and they were coming to kill us." He continued to put the night in perspective: "We were drinking coffee, and we heard on the radio that the penitentiary was under the control of the inmates. Everybody started to block their doors. And we heard, all of a sudden, a hissing noise. It must have been a cutter that they were cutting through Cellblock Four. It was just kind of hysterical."

According to Michael Washburn, "About four o'clock we started seeing police cars pull up. . . . We were flashing SOSs with our lights, trying to get those cops to come in and they wouldn't come in. The guys on the other side, on the north side, were hollering, 'Hey! They're cutting into [Four]. They're killing motherfuckers.'" Washburn went on: "The state troopers were parked all up and down the fence, man. You could see them driving inside the sally port. Why didn't they come in? The back door was right there."

Fuentes described the actions of the more desperate inmates. "It was still dark outside. Then Jim Gossens was hollering and burning his mattress; it got real smoky." Others also saw Gossens burning materials in his cell, in order to create a smoke screen. Most inmates, however, stayed stunned. Finally, they began barricading their cells in preparation for what was inevitable.

David Peterson described the desperate attempts. "After a while I took my bunk and wedged it between the bars and I tied it with rags to secure my door. Then I stood there and I watched them; I was trying to evaluate how long that torch had to run. I was assuming that they could possibly be those workers—you know, who were working in Five. They maybe just had one tank or something like that; it takes about two tanks to one acetylene. I wasn't aware that they had the whole penitentiary."

It was, at the latest, 4:00 in the morning. The acetylene torches hissed through those early hours. By sunrise, the steel door separating Cellblock Four from the main corridor fell from its hinges. Four hours had passed.

Washburn said, "Have you ever heard an acetylene torch when it drops and hits the ground and makes that boom? That big sound? That's what happened. They said, 'They're here.'"

"And then the door popped open," Melvin Thomas said. "And they come running and said, 'You punks and snitches, we're going to kill every one of you.'"

As was true in the other cellblocks, all doors could be opened from the outside—from a control system usually manned by the porters. By turning bedframes vertically and sticking the steel legs in between the cell bars, prisoners could block the door from opening. In the past, this had been a point of contention with correctional officers, allowing them probable cause to have an entire cellblock put on lockdown. For protective custody inmates it now was the only saving grace. Inmate David Peterson explained his other efforts. "I had a mattress folded over, doubled, and then I had a couple of blankets bunched up in that area where the mattress was at. And a couple of legal manilla envelopes, large ones."

Whatever auditory horrors the night had held were becoming human-formed. With dawn rising their faceless presence was replaced first by a dash of bizarre outfits and veils, stocking masks, pillowcases with handmade eyelets—some with jagged, single holes—cyclops made in haste. Then riot gear helmets and beanies and, in one case, a regulation-sized American flag, torn from the wall of the guard's office and made into a poncho—the madness of this parade only outdone by the weapons they held. The tear gas guns. The hundreds of homemade shanks. Police batons and shields, bedposts, metal rods found on the backs of certain chairs in the visitation room. There were industrial kitchen utensils of all kinds, from two-foot-long bread knives to meat-tenderizing mallets to an enormous paddle used to stir vats of soup and stew. And still they carried with them, they trudged behind them, the acetylene torches. The killing squads were not done.

The first death squad marched through the vestibule and onto the middle tier, north side, around 8:00 that morning. Ironically, they passed cell 29, near the front doors, which was home to Chilly Willie, a notorious snitch so derided by the general population that he was more or less considered a member of the administration. He managed to hide until the group passed him, at which point he could not help himself: he grabbed a small mirror and looked down the line. The group split in half: one began chasing Michael Briones, Willie's neighbor, down the tier. The other group amassed outside of cell 25, home to an inmate named Ramon Madrid (no relation to Joe, the murdered E-1 resident).

At forty, Ramon was the oldest fatality of the riot; by that February night Madrid had been inside the prison for five years, doing time as a habitual burglar who stole to finance a heroin addiction. Paul Casaus, Henry Clark, and an inmate identified only as Marcy headed directly for Madrid's cell. Casaus, whose last name is a medieval form of Casas and who was described as a güero, donned a riot helmet and a tear gas launcher. At cell 25, Ramon pleaded with Casaus not to hurt him. Madrid told Casaus he had papers in his cell proving that Madrid hadn't snitched on Casaus. Casaus fired a tear gas grenade into Ramon's stomach. "Get up, bro," he shouted. "Tell me," he said, and shot Ramon again, twice this time. "Tell me where these papers are at."

But this inmate Marcy, according to Willie, instigated the death blow. "He said, 'I'm from Las Cruces. Este puto es rata. Kill him.' I had the mirror out. . . . I was looking out when I saw that motherfucker shoot him again and again." Ramon's body was dragged halfway outside of his cell. There, the group, now joined by an inmate named Richard Buzbee, took an aerosol spray can of Right Guard deodorant and used it to light Ramon Madrid on fire. Buzbee, a morbidly obese inmate with a Santa Claus beard, a rapist and sadist whose voice changed to a whiny trill when violence became likely, found another can of Right Guard and tossed another homemade incendiary onto Ramon's body.

This was not the first instance in which a tear gas grenade was used as a weapon. Earlier, in Cellblock Three, the same group had used this method in an attack on Juan Sanchez. Sanchez was a Mexican National, nicknamed Poncho Villa by other inmates. He had an undiagnosed mental condition and tended toward unprovoked attacks on other inmates. He had no connections, no cliques, no sympathy from correctional officers, which he was known to attack as well. He never made it out of his cell. Inmates struck him multiple times between the bars with tear gas grenades. It killed Sanchez, and forced any inmates in Cellblock Three who aimed to wait out the riot in their cells to rush into the central corridor, gagging and temporarily blind.

At the same time Ramon Madrid was being set on fire with aerosol cans in Cellblock Four, inmate David Peterson witnessed an attack unfold on Michael Briones, Willie's neighbor:

When they broke in[to] Cellblock Four I went behind the bunk. I was in a crouch. Still at the time I didn't know they had the whole joint. They started snuffing people. The first one they snuffed was right in front of my cell, they snuffed him and he had it. They was beating him down the run.

■ ■ ■

Michael Briones, a twenty-two-year-old from Albuquerque convicted of rape, was three months shy of his first parole hearing. Something had occurred in the medical unit between Michael Briones and another inmate named Andy Gonzales, which had landed Briones in Cellblock Four. When the first announcements of the riot came to the cellblock, Briones broke a piece of his steel bed railing and sat on the floor, furiously sharpening it against the cold concrete. He'd only managed to sharpen the bedpost halfway when Lonnie Valdez, Moises Sandoval—known as Troca—and Andy Gonzales appeared outside of his door. Because Briones had chosen to use his bed as a defensive weapon rather than a locking mechanism, one of the men called out, "Twenty-eight!" and the door rolled open. Willie described what happened next. "Briones got on top of the rail and tried to pull himself up to the third tier on the north side when someone hit him with a pipe, and he let go. From there he jumped from the middle tier down to the bottom tier and was met by Moises Sandoval. Sandoval said, 'Pescame ese puto por que me lo voy matar, me lo voy chingar.' And then Moises started running after Michael Briones, and Briones dropped that flat bar he had made to use as a knife.

"He ran from the northwest corner of the north side of the building to the south side of the building, which is when he met up with Andy Gonzales. Andy met him at the corner and hit him with a pipe in the back of the head and several times in the back. Briones kept running. He ran all the way to the west side of the building; started climbing up the bars; he was still on the south side and he fell; and he fell right there in the southwest corner of the building on the south side, which [is where] Moises Sandoval and Andy Gonzales killed Michael Briones."

Briones was not the last inmate to fall to the basement. Michael Washburn watched a group led by Bobby "Barbershop" Garcia kill Leo Tenorio. "They stomped Leo out of his cell. He tried to jump over the railing to get out, to run away. He fell off the third tier. He fell on his head. There's a wall with the radiator and pipe coming out. The dude hit his head on the pipe. That alone probably would've broken his neck. He was sitting there, twitching. Then that little Mexican dude [Barbershop] pulled out a bed and dropped it down on his head. Blood going everywhere. Leo was dead by then, I guess. But I saw Reggie Bell beat Leo in the face with a pipe to make sure."

Before lunchtime, a third body, that of Phillip Hernandez, would be tossed down into the basement. Hernandez was doing eighteen months for unlawful entry. He'd been given probation on the matter for turning state's witness against men named Ricky Chavez and Lorenzo Chavez (unrelated) in a homicide in Clovis 1978. But when his probation was revoked, Hernandez found himself inside the same institution as the Chavez pair. He was immediately assigned to protective custody. Ricky Chavez and Lorenzo Chavez were soon joined by Troca, Richard Buzbee, Paul Casaus and his tear gas launcher, as well as an inmate named Narciso Flores. Within minutes they'd beaten and stabbed Phillip Hernandez, tossing his body from the middle tier to join Briones and Tenorio. He landed near Michael Briones, who, despite the viciousness of his attack, was still breathing. David Peterson, who lived in the cell directly across from where Briones had fallen, told State Police the inmate laid in front of his cell for four hours, breathing. "He received several beatings from various groups that came through," Peterson said.

The witness said the whole Briones affair came to an end finally when Michael Colby and William Jack Stephens arrived in Cellblock Four. They'd waited while others dealt with the tedium of the torch, spending the early morning hours shooting liquid Valium. Now that the block was open, Colby and Stephens, after a brief reconnoiter in the kitchen for armament, strolled into the protective unit. "'We're here to help you,' they said to Michael Briones. 'We're police officers.' And then commenced to beating on his ass." Peterson claimed that a psychological block prevented him from naming who exactly found Briones's makeshift shank, but one of the two, Peterson claimed, watching from six feet away, drove the piece of steel through Briones's left ear and into his skull. The jagged end came out near the lower jaw on the right side of his face, forcing his jaw open and his tongue to hang out. He was left like that for investigators to find.

Amid this garden of hell, a surreal moment transpired. A twenty-four-year-old kid wandered into Cellblock Four alone, totally tranquilized. His name was Joseph Mirabal. He'd been married at nineteen to a seventeen-year-old bride. His parole hearing was scheduled for April—less than ninety days away. He claimed Alamogordo as his hometown. Given that Mirabal was classified as medium-security and worked in food services and was housed in an honors dormitory, he was of no great threat to the institution or to the public. Mirabal likely began the standard regimen for nervous inmates: chlorpromazine. Known by its brand name, Thorazine, the medication is used to treat paranoid schizophrenia, bipolar disorder, and violent impulses. Side effects include vomiting and dizziness, but most commonly Thorazine users are known for troubled and labored breathing, a dead shuffle-walk, and a general absence of fear for pain.

Somehow, Joseph Mirabal had managed to tranquilize himself; this might've been okay, but the Thorazine caused him to shuffle aimlessly from the safety of his dorm and into Cellblock Four of his own accord. The screaming and shouting, the hollering and cursing, it stopped immediately. Both the death squads and their potential victims paused to take in the strange sight. James Peterson saw him. "There's a little bit [of a closet space between cells] 90 and 89. There was a mattress. Now what happened there, there was a Spanish fellow, he comes stumbling like he was loaded on pills and he was just like dead and his eyes were . . . he looked like he was out on pills. He comes stumbling down to about my cell and I was ducked [down]. He comes stumbling up and somebody asked him what unit are you from and all of that. Then they told him to lay down on this mattress. They dragged him and put him on this mattress. They finally beat him to death."

Mirabal, too, had his body thrown down into the basement.

Jammed cells were proving only to delay the inevitable. On the middle tier, two Anglo inmates—one known as "Grandpa" Larry Smith and one, the panicking inmate who'd set fire to his mattress, Donald Gossens— were slowly and helplessly watching their cell bars give way to the torches.

Larry Smith was a notorious informant. From Farmington, New Mexico, Smith had participated in an armed robbery that'd turned deadly, with the shooting of a gas station clerk. Smith told investigators that Richard Nave Chapman was the brains behind the scheme, which led both him and Chapman to the same prison. Smith's cellblock neighbor and best friend, James Arnold Kilker, who'd known Smith for decades going back to their time in a county lockup in Colorado, told State Police that he was sitting on his bed when the death squads appeared on the middle tier. Kilker said six to eight inmates passed his cell and surrounded Smith's. The group included Richard Nave Chapman, Richard Buzbee, James Humiston, and, eventually, Michael Colby. Buzbee spoke to Smith and then shouted, "We got a tough punk here! Get the torch."

Over a dozen inmates told State Police that aside from a state-issued navy beanie and his aviators, Colby hardly cared to disguise himself. Again and again, inmates referenced him in the "baseball bat murder." They mentioned William Jack "Two Pack" Stephens as well; Stephens had gone to the trouble of tying a bandanna around his neck but was too stoned, too arrogant, or too unperturbed to care, and so it hung around his neck, acting as no more than an Old West–style kerchief.

Smith's neighbor Kilker told investigators that Colby spoke with Smith for a while. He ultimately told Smith: "Don't ask for mercy now, punk," and called upon Buzbee and his crew to torch the cell door. "I stood on a chair," Kilker said, "and I looked at Larry Smith. He was sitting on his toilet. The bed was propped against the bars. They couldn't even get in and he had his bars tied down with towels and rags and stuff. And he kind of gave me an up, his palm up, like, 'What can I do?' There was nothing I could do to get him out."

Smith waited at his toilet while the group opened his cell. The process took half an hour. By all accounts, Richard Buzbee spat the most vicious bile at inmates awaiting their deaths. "Buzbee was still talking to the dude," Kilker said. "'I've got you, punk! You can't get away now, you snitching little dog.' All sorts of crap like that." Kilker explained what he saw once the cell bars had been burned away: "He [Larry Smith] started swinging. He stood up on the toilet and reached into the sink and pulled out [a weapon]. He hit one of the inmates. And he was fighting, swinging at the rest. And he got hit with a pipe. Another guy hit him with something. And then that little fat motherfucker Buzbee went and hit him with a hammer. Buzbee hit him a good one in the side of the head. Smith just fell back and hit the toilet. His head hit the toilet. Then they were on him. I seen them light the torch again, and I knew what they were going to do then. He started screaming, man. Buzbee burned him for a while. They were burning [Smith's] dick and nuts. Then they cooked his face." A later autopsy performed by the state noted that one of Larry Smith's testicles had been shoved down his throat.

At this time, inmate Vincent Romero managed to free himself from his cell. The merit of being locked behind your own door was quickly waning; these death squads allowed inmates in Four to leave their cells if they were recognized by somebody on the line, or if they promised to participate. Whatever the case with Vincent Romero, the arrangement was not honored. No sooner had he come out of his cell than he was stabbed by another inmate, at least a half dozen times. An eyewitness reported: "Out of adrenaline flow, Romero had a lot of strength and was trying to get to the end of the tier to get away. But when they got to around cell 25, he kind of put his arms down, like he was ready to drop." Romero was dead, but his body was not left unperturbed. He was hanged from a tier with a rope and left there.

Before lunchtime, the bodies of Ramon Madrid, Larry Smith, and Joe Mirabal, the kid who'd wandered into Four, were on fire. Michael Briones, Leo Tenorio, Phillip Hernandez, and Joe Mirabal lay in the basement. Tenorio was still alive. As inmates Michael Colby and Reggie Bell rained steel bedframes down upon these basement victims, Leo Tenorio was doing what he could to avoid the crashing frames. He twitched. He moved slightly out of the way. The blood loss had made his actions largely instinctive. His head was eventually crushed by a bedframe.

Finally, around lunchtime, the door to Donald Gossens's cell gave way. Donald Gossens had been at Old Main for six weeks, following an attempted sale of amphetamines. He had a two-and-a-half-year-old daughter at home; his birthday had been the night before. Gossens, like most nonviolent inmates, had been attracted to the notion of shorter sentencing or early parole in exchange for information on trafficking within the prison. A half dozen inmates surrounded his cell door.

His neighbor, Michael Washburn, had been set free by a member of the Aryan Brotherhood. "I know when the guys came in, the little white dude said [to Gossens], 'You got me a life sentence, motherfucker! I'm gonna fuck you up and then I'm gonna beat you to death.'" Despite being unable to identify the assailants, Washburn said the clan stayed true to their word, using rubber-mallet hammers to kill Gossens.

At the same time, Reggie Bell and his squad gathered outside the cell of Mario Daniel Urioste. Known as Junior, Urioste was five foot two and weighed 110 pounds. The Urioste family had long but unceremonious connections to the land, the paterfamilias having been among the first few conquistador foot soldiers to have moved the entire family to the New World. Junior was small and pale. He lived with his mother. Only weeks before February 1, 1980, Urioste had been arrested for stealing fly-fishing equipment from a local sporting goods store. His mother was too poor to pay his bail and so, while awaiting trial on a misdemeanor charge of shoplifting, Junior had been sent to Old Main. Within the first forty-eight hours of his time at the maximum-security institution, Urioste was gang-raped. He demanded to press charges; for that, he was sent to Cellblock Four.

On the morning of the riot, Junior was housed in cell 5, top tier, northside. Melvin Thomas's cell was six cells to the west. Thomas identified two men, Bruce Lorenzo and Reggie Bell, as the men who went after Junior Urioste. Inmate Lorenzo had a pipe bender. He also wore a riot helmet, while Bell, who weighed around 235 pounds, wore a riot helmet and had equipped himself with an ingenuously vicious tool. According to a number of witnesses, Bell had found a long piece of steel, a pole, to which he'd bonded a homemade shank. It was a weapon with foresight, long enough to stick inmates who cowered against the back walls or dark corners of their cells. There wasn't enough weight, enough momentum, to make these jabs lethal; instead it became a form of bloodletting torture.

Melvin Thomas told State Police: "There were three or four dudes in front of Junior's cell. 'Get him open. He's a punk. We're gonna fuck him. Let's take him in here and fuck him.' They took him into an office, and used him." (The office Thomas is referring to would have been the correctional officers' and porters' tiny closet-like office, where files and photographs of those on the block were held. Of course, in Old Main fashion, these photographs were rarely updated to account for transfers, deaths, paroles, or changes in classification within the prison. It was a useless infographic, except for when it was not. Then, it lent vengeful inmates to the exact locations of their victims.) Thomas told State Police that he did not see what happened inside of the office, but by the time the assailants left, Junior was dead. "I didn't see them kill him, but when Reggie Bell walked out, he said, 'I got mine. I got mine.'" Thomas said he tried to look into the office but paperwork had been set on fire. Nonetheless, he could make out Urioste's feet sticking out from behind a desk.

After this, both Reggie Bell's death squad and Colby and Stephens's squad met outside the cell of James Perrin.

James Delbert Perrin had lived a lonely life. He split rent with his sister, was obese, suffered from a low IQ, and spent his time on the road as a semitruck driver. He loved to listen to music on the radio, and the lengthy drives provided for him the solace with which he felt most comfortable. Other inmates thought he was weird, and it did not help that Perrin had found himself at Old Main through a series of misfortunes. Outside of his hometown of Chaparral, a lonely place of sixteen thousand leaned up against the steppes of the Llano Estacado, Perrin began hanging out with a younger guy named Jimmy Kinslow. Kinslow, a tall and attractive man of the Chickasaw Nation in Oklahoma, was later known for a wild prison break in 1987, from Old Main, which included a dozen hardened criminals, a helicopter, and interstate trips spent on the top of semitruck trailers. Kinslow was a rapist and murderer, a robber who talked Perrin into helping him kill a woman named Patricia Andrews in Chaparral. Her two daughters were also killed. Despite Perrin having a solid alibi, he was sent to Cellblock Four as a child rapist and murderer. Today, it is believed that Perrin was innocent. That didn't matter on the day of the riot.

An eyewitness told State Police: "Colby was hunting for Perrin." When asked to identify Colby, Melvin Thomas said, "He had the hat on, but it was frizzed underneath. His hair was reddish-blondish color. He had on two-toned Levi's." Inmate Michael Washburn told a similar story: "When I got out of my cell I walked by and I saw them fucking up Gossens . . . and I kind of looked at that for a second. As soon as I saw they were killing Gossens, I stepped out. And I saw another guy. He was a tall white dude with a mustache, had sunglasses on, and he had light blue jeans with a different color, a lighter blue in them. He was trying to get Jim Perrin."

Like Larry Smith, it took inmates nearly a half hour to burn into James Perrin's cell. While Smith had spent that time waiting and armed, Perrin chose to spend his final minutes singing the Eagles' 1975 hit "Take It to the Limit." Inmate Jimmy Mims watched his final, agonizing seconds. "First, they burned his eyes out. Then they cut his tongue out with the cutting torch. Then after that, they just . . . oh, lord, they gave it to him good. They beat him, stabbed him."

■ ■ ■

Perhaps the most notorious homicide to come out of the riot was that of Paulina Paul. A Black man who suffered from schizophrenia, paranoia, a persecutory complex, and other undiagnosed mental illnesses, Paul had no allies. He was loathed by not only the general population but by his fellow inmates inside of Cellblock Four. He often went unclothed and smeared feces on the walls of his cell. Sometimes he told his neighbors he was Christ. Often he simply screamed. He would stand for an hour or so in his cell and scream. Many of his outbursts were racially motivated. He blamed white people for his problems. Anglo and Chicano inmates often joined up for a common cause, but it was almost unheard of for either of these groups to affiliate themselves with the Black population—who were viewed as untrustworthy, and given their small numbers, they relied on administration for protection. The vast majority of Black inmates at Old Main found an exit from the prison early and spent the majority of the riot in the yard, talking with police stationed outside of the perimeter. But Paul was also hated by Black inmates. To be connected with Paulina Paul meant exposure to relentless violence before the riot began—to say nothing of trying to protect him during the break in Cellblock Four. Reggie Bell and Lorenzo Bruce, the two outlier Black inmates accused of violence during the melee, knew Paulina Paul would be snuffed out by Anglos before nightfall on Saturday. They offered no help, no bargaining on behalf of Paulina's life.

The riot was interpreted as a catalyst by all cliques inside the penitentiary, but exactly what it meant for the future differed radically by group. The most progressive, legitimate inmate group was led by Lonnie Duran—and later by his cousin, Dwight. Comprised largely of jailhouse lawyers, former professionals, and inmates associated with La Raza and the civil rights movement, they quickly followed Lonnie Duran's call for negotiations with the state. He'd been the lead plaintiff in a 1977 complaint aimed at Governor Jerry Apodaca. To the astonishment of many, the court sided with Lonnie Duran and the inmates represented in the civil suit. The suit is formally named *Duran v. Apodaca*, but it is known more widely as the Duran Consent Decree. It is a milestone case, one that protects inmates to this day. Duran argued against the state on thirteen matters: correspondence regulations, general visitation, attorney visitation, food service, inmate legal access, classification, living conditions, inmate activity, medical care, mental health care, staffing and training, maximum security, and inmate discipline. New Mexico had been found neglectful in all thirteen of these matters, and there was reason to celebrate for those inmates who earnestly believed the system would be corrected.

By the time of the riot, none of the changes in the decree had been implemented. Lonnie and his associates were more than happy for the riot to have broken out because it allowed the entire nation to see the mishandling of inmates. On the other hand, this group avoided violence. In fact, one prisoner, a medical doctor, began helping injured correctional officers and was later thanked with saving lives. Duran's group asked for media attention. For this reason media attention became one of the more vital keys in hostage negotiations.

Unfortunately for Duran, by the time his negotiation demands were relayed to law enforcement, other cliques had already made demands—many of them fatuous. Inmates corroborated this to the New Mexico State Police, postriot. Inmate David Fuentes said he and a few inmates had managed to find their way to the mess hall and scavenge something to eat when Donald Stout approached them. Stout told the group he'd been outside in the yard, but that he only had a list of four demands thus far. "I need more sensible demands." As Sue DeWalt told me, the initial demands were scattered and frivolous. Prison psychologist Dr. Marc Orner agreed. "I want you to write this down," he told me, "because nobody has ever mentioned it. Not the press, not any writers. The first list of demands, do you know what they were?" I told Orner that I did: steak dinners and a pool table in every dormitory. "That's right!" Orner said. "*This* is what they were after."

Lonnie Duran had to fight for his legitimacy: with every trivial item added, he had to begin again in assuring the administration and the state that the inmates were more than simply wreaking havoc. He spent a majority of the riot having to undo the threats of violence spoken to authorities over the radio by somebody named Chopper One. This pseudonym took on a mysterious lore of its own, with many of those involved in the case postriot believing the identity of Chopper One could lead to the unraveling of mysterious forces. The truth was that Chopper One was not an inmate; rather, it was any number of inmates who grabbed a radio and announced intentions to the outside. Despite all of the chaos and downright false impressions, law enforcement stayed adamant that they had a handle on matters inside the pen so long as they spoke to Lonnie.

For William Jack Stephens and Michael Colby, only later, while appearing on television, would the pair associate themselves with Lonnie Duran's mission for reform. The truth was the riot offered them a chance to consolidate power. Throughout the ordeal, Colby and Stephens met more than one white inmate willing to prove himself fit for this new brotherhood. Inmate Buddy Gammons told the New Mexico State Police about a conversation he had about the initiation process. Gammons said he ran into Richard Buzbee in dormitory C-1. Gammons asked him what was going on. "'Well,' [Buzbee] said, 'everything's cool because I just hit four of them in Cellblock Four for my initiation into the brotherhood.' I asked him what he meant. He said, 'Yeah, I got four snitches and killed all four of 'em.'"

Another inmate eager to prove his worth to the brotherhood was James "Tex" French, a six-foot-tall cowboy with ties to Arizona. It'd been while at Florence that French first picked up a reputation as a snitch; he'd turned state's witness on a planned race riot. After testifying, French was moved to New Mexico and placed in Cellblock Four, on the north side, top tier. His cell was next to Paulina Paul's.

Melvin Thomas was also housed on the same tier, in cell 12. He witnessed the arrival of Michael Colby and William Jack Stephens on the north side. Thomas knew Michael Colby from county lockup in Bernalillo. Colby passed his cell, noting Thomas vaguely and then leaving him alone. "He came down the run with, it looked like to me, a carving knife in his hand about eighteen inches long." David Fuentes also told investigators Colby was carrying a cleaver from the kitchen, and guessed it to be "about three foot long." Another Cellblock Four inmate named Jesse Lovato told State Police that "one of them had a bread-cutting knife about a foot and a half long. Colby had that. Michael Colby had that bread knife."

In a second, follow-up interview, when asked to elaborate on the subject of Colby's weapon, Fuentes told authorities: "Its length was around two feet. It was pretty wide. It was a machete-looking object. It was sharp and chrome-plated and it had a black handle."

They arrived outside of James French's cell to kill him. The group included Colby, William Jack Stephens, Daryl Jean Stelly, and Michael Price as well as inmates John Howard and Jesse Trujillo—Trujillo being the inmate who assisted in the escape and had stabbed eighty-one-year-old Richard Dew while on the lam in Santa Fe. James French begged them for mercy. They told French he could save himself by killing his neighbor, Paulina Paul. Colby handed him the meat cleaver. (When asked how many killings this group had participated in, David Fuentes said, "They were the ones that were mainly doing all the killing.")

Inmate Melvin Thomas told State Police he was responsible for opening Paul's cell. He said he helped out an inmate named Pete Flores, who was marked for death, and then did the same for Paul, so that Paul could find some way to run. Thomas said that not long after, Moises Sandoval stepped inside cell 23, home to Elias Jaramillo. "This Moises dude . . . was hanging the guy in cell 23. The guy in cell 23 had done been, his head was done busted open, his stomach had been cut, but [Moises] was still hanging him anyway." The attorney general's report would later list the cause of death for Jaramillo as hanging.

While this occurred, James French entered Paulina Paul's cell. According to Melvin Thomas, "They knew that Tex was a snitch or whatever. They says, 'If you want to live, go in there and kill this guy and we'll let you live.' Tex went in there."

French was unable to complete the job. Most eyewitnesses corroborate what Melvin Thomas later told authorities: "[Colby] had this cleaver. He said, 'You mean you all can't kill this punk?' He said, 'I'll show you how to kill this punk! Get his head! Pull him up here.' Colby turned his back to us. They had the man's hair, they had him by the back of the head. His throat was tight. The cleaver swung and pulled back. He said, 'That's how you kill a punk,' and walked away."

Paulina Paul was decapitated, and whereas others killed inside Cellblock Four were left with the small dignity of remaining where they'd been housed, Paul's torso and head were paraded through nearly the entire institution. Michael Price placed Paul's head on the end of a broomstick and left Four; he went out into the main corridor, opened his fly, and, with one hand parading the head on the broomstick and the other massaging his penis, laughed.

Paul's head was then carried to Cellblock One, to show the old men and honor inmates what they could expect if they dared to leave their block. Ultimately, Paul's body and head were left outside of the Catholic chapel. (After the riot New Mexico State Police Officer Susan DeWalt was forced to see the body. "The National Guard had me come up to a victim beneath a sheet. They asked me, 'You know this guy?' and pulled the sheet back. Paulina's head was between his knees. The Guard thought it was funny. They wanted to see what a woman would do seeing a decapitation. They might've taken bets on me passing out." DeWalt told them she didn't know the inmate and went back to her work.)

The State Police pinned the murder on French, who was in for twenty to one hundred years for rape. While interviewing him, French claimed he was set up because of his involvement in an attempted uprising in Arizona a few years prior. "I's allegedly 'posed to been involved in this race riot . . . in Florence. Two prison guards were brutally murdered, and I was accused of going to turn state's witness, which I did not. When I came here Deputy Warden Montoya says, 'I know who you are, and I know about the riot, and there is only one way you will get out of this prison, and that's [with] a tag on your fuckin' feet.'"

One of the few claims made by Colby and Stephens postriot was that they had lost friends, as well. They mentioned Tom O'Meara and Kelly

Johnson. Along with Filiberto Ortega, these inmates were found in the gymnasium, their bodies burned so badly it would take the rest of the month for them to be identified by way of dental records. Ortega had been a dormmate with Jeff Williams in B-1, as had been Filiberto's younger brother, Frank. Before the riot, Frank, doing time for murder but up for a parole hearing in October 1980, told his mother on the phone he did not expect to make it that long. Frank's body, beaten to death, was removed from the premises and into the yard by inmates on the final day of the riot. There, his body lay with Richard Fierro's, who'd been tossed out into the yard around 6:50 on the first morning of the riot.

As for Kelly Johnson and Tom O'Meara: O'Meara had been at the penitentiary a short time; he'd been interviewed for a documentary called *Doing Time* mere weeks before the riot. He was an attractive young blond with a mustache. Johnson was also an attractive young man, a dropout from the US Army who'd gotten mixed up in a large forgery ring in Albuquerque. His parents waited for over a month to learn of his fate. His body had been burned to the point that it was the last to be found, nearly mistaken for rubble.

The most severely pillaged unit beyond Cellblock Four was dormitory F-1, where Richard Fierro had been housed. He was not the only victim from the unit. Robert L. Rivera, a twenty-six-year-old forger from Carlsbad, had been asked to participate in the riot. When he declined, an acquaintance from the streets stabbed him once, in the heart. Rivera died nearly immediately; his body was left in the central corridor. Aside from Richard Fierro and Robert Rivera, Ben Moreno, Gilbert Moreno, and Robert Quintela all died during the riot. These victims were all from Carlsbad. Ben and Gilbert Moreno were cousins. Gilbert Moreno's body was found inside the control center after; according to the attorney general's office, a police officer stepped on his body while breeching the control center through a broken window. Robert Quintela's body was found there, too, beaten and stabbed. Ben Moreno, who had had his skull crushed, was removed from the institution by inmates around breakfast on February 3.

Finally, in F-1, an inmate named Russell Werner, a twenty-two-year-old armed robber from Albuquerque, succumbed to carbon monoxide poisoning. His body lay in the hallway when unknown inmates, armed with one of the acetylene torches, decided to burn his corpse. What remained was beaten and Werner's skull destroyed. His charred body was left inside the otherwise untouched Catholic chapel.

The second most brutalized dormitory was A-1, an honors unit. These murders were likely due to proximate location to E-2, where the riot began. Dorm F was next to E and directly across from A. The deaths here are far more difficult to elucidate than those in Cellblock Four. Like Joseph Mirabal, inmates James Foley and Danny Waller were housed in A-1. While Mirabal, drugged, had let himself into the bloodiest cellblock of the riot, Waller and Foley died where they had lived.

James Christopher Foley proved to be the youngest victim of the riot: at nineteen, he'd done time for stealing cars, but in November 1979 he'd been convicted of the murder of a Circle K employee. His appeal was still pending, and he'd been transferred from Cellblock Four to A-1 on January 30. He was beaten, suffered massive craniocerebral injuries, and was carried out to the South Tower, where he died shortly thereafter.

Daniel Dewayne Waller was from Lubbock and had come to Old Main for credit card fraud. Waller's death offers another wrinkle to the killings within the penitentiary. Though Michael Colby's statement to New Mexico State Police is contradictory and self-interested, he displayed the intelligence of a lifelong convict when he distinguished the two main types of killings: grudge killings and informant killings. Waller's death, according to an inmate who witnessed the assault and spoke to the *Albuquerque Tribune*, was a prolonged matter. The A-1 eyewitness stated that Waller had gone out into the central corridor, only to return soon thereafter with lacerations to his skull. Other A-1 inmates tended to him. But Danny had at some point made a stop at the pharmacy, and by the time he arrived back at A-1, he was feeling hardly any pain. He stayed in A-1. Waller didn't notice, but the population within his dorm changed rather quickly: those who'd helped him earlier soon left, to be replaced by inmates who wanted to use the dorm as a place to commit rape. The inmate who'd spoke to the *Tribune* detailed his final moments. "Later he was running around the dorm shooting off his mouth about how he had broken into the wardrobe in the gym and was wearing a flashy shirt and other inmates kept trying to get it from him. Waller had a large shank and kept scaring them away." Finally, the inmate claimed three others lying around the cell tired of his antics. "They started stabbing and laughing at the same time. This was a wanton killing."

Wanton killings can account for Juan Sanchez, the Mexican National; Richard Fierro; and Richard Rivera, who was stabbed, eyewitnesses later said, deeper into the chest cavity than his assailant meant. There were also the murders of Joseph Mirabal, Lawrence Cardon, and Robert Quintela. Inmates caught in the corridor or in the wrong unit at the wrong time were open to the primeval desire to quell rage after a half decade of mistreatment and resentment.

The killing of informants was an inevitable outcome of the PNM's means of control. By pitting inmates against each other and offering the only safety in a cell unit twenty-five yards from those that had been accused, the administration provided no protection. While these killings certainly entered into a state of wanton, they were entirely led by rioting inmates who told others the victim was a rat. Michael Colby told the BBC, "That was over with before noon, Saturday. Whatever happened in there happened, and was done." The BBC told Colby he had been accused of killing in Cellblock Four. "Were you in Cellblock Four?" they asked. "I've been in Cellblock Four before, yeah," Colby responded.

■ ■ ■

Negotiations to end the riot had begun within an hour of the breach in the central command center. Deputy Warden Robert Montoya, Superintendent of Correctional Security Manuel Koroneos, and Warden Jerry Griffin all had homes on the grounds and were the first to convene at the guardhouse just outside the front entrance of the penitentiary. They were soon joined by Marc Orner.

Psychologist Marc Orner was asleep at his condo in Santa Fe when his phone rang. It was Warden Montoya. Around 6:40, he joined the ersatz headquarters and began to radio inmates inside. Orner was there to help identify voices and nicknames. Of the officials inside the gatehouse, Marc Orner was least alarmed by what they witnessed. He knew what was happening. He'd warned everybody already, and now he found himself playing a brutal game in which his prophecies had been realized.

Dr. Marc Orner served as the director of psychological services at the Corrections Department from 1973 to 1981. Originally from Philadelphia, he received a PhD in counseling psychology from the University of New Mexico before returning east to serve as a postdoctoral fellow at the Albert Einstein College of Medicine in the Bronx. He then took a job as a schoolteacher and then as the school's counselor. But Marc Orner was not happy in the city. When a position opened at the Penitentiary of New Mexico, Orner jumped at the chance. At just twenty-nine and with no prior experience in corrections, he was placed in charge of counseling services.

Less than a year into his new job, Orner was forced to act as a hostage negotiator during a twenty-two-hour standoff involving a parole violator who had taken an eighty-four-year-old man hostage in a farmhouse. Orner had no background or expertise in such a role; administration decided he was fit for the job because he had treated the suspect in the past (the negotiations were ultimately successful). Soon into his tenure he began an in-depth group and individual therapy regimen for sexual offenders, later telling the *New Mexican* that it was "the finest sexual dysfunction program in the Rocky Mountains."

Still, 1973 was not a good year for rehabilitative proponents. Aside from budget slashes and the impossible demands placed upon him, Dr. Orner also ran into resistance to his practices from his superiors, who did not trust him. They'd hired him out of deference to the legislature, who had wanted an outside view of the prison's operations. Orner was offering alternatives to the mainstream, mass incarceration theory that'd taken over the national ethos. But the hostility toward the clinician went beyond simple nepotism, and tapped into an animosity unique to the culture of northern New Mexico.

Though Santa Fe is known for its ski lodges and artistic ambiance, it is a town of fewer than fifty thousand permanent residents, many of whom come from a few dozen families with ties to land grants dating prior to the arrival of the *Mayflower*. The year 1979 was not far removed from the Chicano movement of the late 1960s, which had had a deep resonance within the northern counties of New Mexico. In the early 1960s, Cesar Chavez and Dolores Huerta had founded the National Farm Workers Association in California, a bold and political movement resolved to better the horrific labor and civil rights violations of Mexican National and Mexican American agriculture workers. Among the movement's primary interests were land rights. This latter issue struck at the heart of unspoken, deep hostilities in New Mexico. The Treaty of Guadalupe Hidalgo, signed in 1848, ended the Mexican-American War in the United States' favor, but guaranteed that certain land grants that had been offered to families within the region—grants that dated back centuries and had been signed initially by the Spanish crown and then honored by the Mexican government—would continue to be honored. These grants essentially promised many communities the rights to the land into perpetuity, giving them an exceptional form of sovereignty while also allowing these communities to be granted immediate US citizenship. While this last point held true, the United States almost immediately began to ignore the land grants; by the 1960s, none of them held legal sway—not in any true sense. Decades of influx by Anglos, who took farms from families with the backing of the federal and state governments, sparked the land protest movement of 1967. Led by Chicano activist Reies Tijerina, the protests became violent when Tijerina's aliancistas raided the Rio Arriba courthouse and shot two law officers. To this day in Rio Arriba, old billboards can be found with Emiliano Zapata's visage and the protest's battle cry: ¡Tierra o Muerte!

An uneasy truce between Anglos and Chicanos pervaded the succeeding years. Both sides had a common antagonist: outsiders. By the mid-1970s, Hollywood producers, actors, and wealthy guru types began showing up in the little town and buying property. This in turn caused real estate prices and monthly rents to skyrocket, leaving Santa Feans resentful that their own backyard was now unaffordable. Orner didn't know or understand this until he'd already left New York for Santa Fe. Compounding problems, Orner was averse to genuflection, and his personality was at odds with the mores of northern New Mexico, which values stoicism and plain-speak. Orner wore flamboyant shirts and jewelry and once told the newspaper that inmates were two-time losers. "He terms most inmates as chronically unsuccessful people. 'They are even unsuccessful criminals or [else] they wouldn't be in here,' he said."

Inmates read this interview when it appeared in pages of the *New Mexican* in 1977.

Despite the animosity, those in charge were realizing Orner was the only man they could rely on to discuss issues inside with the inmates in charge. He knew them. The sun not yet risen, Orner told other administrators what he was finding out. Inmates housed in E-2 had let out the inmates in Cellblock Three. This wasn't good. Presuming, however, that the guards assigned to Cellblock Four followed protocol, it was possible for the most vulnerable wing of the prison to be, more or less, quarantined.

It would take a few more hours, until 5:45 that morning, for Deputy Corrections Secretary Felix Rodriguez to join them. He told them he'd been asleep and had not heard the phone ringing. At this point, Rodriguez took command. It was his institution. Both Montoya and Koroneos genuflected to the old boss. Warden Jerry Griffin was new to the facility, having been hired in April 1979—the fifth warden in five years. As the attorney general's report characterizes it, "Griffin was the furthest removed of the decision-makers."

Around this time, Officer Herman Gallegos escaped the penitentiary, becoming the first of the hostages to find freedom. He was helped by sympathetic inmates. This gave the cadre within the gatehouse a tremendous sense of optimism. It meant there were reasonable people still inside; and if the officials could massage the demands the right way, the ordeal could be over soon.

Governor Bruce King arrived at the penitentiary at 8:30 on Saturday morning. He was debriefed in the gatehouse and soon watched as fifty inmates staggered out of a hole they'd cut in the exterior wall of Cellblock Five with an acetylene torch. Officials chose to focus on this promising visual, instead of the audial nightmare emanating from broken windows.

In the meantime, slowly amassing along the perimeter were State Police officers, families of inmates, and the National Guard. Marcella Armijo soon joined a crowd gathering outside the perimeter fence. Her mom had woken her with news that something bad was going on at the pen. "I smelled like booze," Armijo said, "but I stayed there almost twenty-eight hours." The Guard wanted to help but had to await orders. Hours passed. No orders came.

Attica was on Governor Bruce King's mind. Less than a decade earlier, the nation watched in horror as State Police reentered Attica Correctional Facility in an attempt to restore order. In the ensuing melee, forty-three people were killed, including ten officers. King met with prison administrators and discussed what moves could be taken to protect the officers currently held hostage. The hostages, by then, were in various stages of physical injury. Some were unharmed. Others were bleeding out. But all were still alive. If the National Guard stormed the prison, King reasoned, the hostages would be killed. While the governor deliberated, Armijo recalled watching Officer Juan Bustos beaten in front of the Guard and police. "They bring him out and they put him in a chair and make him sit there. And everybody was happy because they were gonna let him go. So they sit him right there [on the steps to the main entrance]. And he's sitting there all beat-up and they start kicking the shit out of him. They start kicking him, punching him, throwing him off the chair. Taunting the administration to do something toward them. That was one of the hardest things to watch, because I couldn't go in."

During negotiations, the first fifty National Guardsmen appeared on the scene. Among them was a young lieutenant named Carlos Martinez, from Taos. Taos is perhaps the most famous of nineteen Pueblo American Indian tribes in New Mexico. For a kid from Taos to serve in the National Guard was to side with the invaders, the US government, against one's own. But Carlos Martinez was strong-willed and not bothered by the resentment. He'd grown up in poverty and watched alcohol and drug addiction ruin the lives of people he loved. He wanted out of these troubles, and the National Guard provided a way. Further, he felt once his enlistment ended he could apply for the police academy in Roswell and return to northern New Mexico in order to serve his community. Any resentment he procured in the meantime would be worth it.

Martinez had no phone or television in his tiny trailer, and so, on February 2, he knew nothing about what was happening down in Santa Fe—not until his father woke him at 8:00 that morning. He told Carlos he was needed in the capital. Martinez listened to the radio during the seventy-mile drive south. Details were still spotty. Something bad was going on at the prison, but that's all anybody knew for certain.

Before arriving, the National Guard had been told they were going to be the entry team to the pen. They should prepare themselves for hand-to-hand combat in a violent retaking of the facility. Upon arrival, the Guard was issued service batons. *Where were their rifles?* they wondered. Most of the members of the battalion had never used batons. An impromptu tutorial began just beyond the prison's perimeter fence.

A persistent demand from the inmates was for the presence of the media. Inmates were especially keen on having the attention of Ernie Mills. Mills was a commentator, a local Paul Harvey; he had a reputation for straight talk and for honesty. The prisoners trusted him. He arrived just before 6:00 that morning and joined in on the radio communications. He spoke with inmates directly. He asked them what was happening and why. They demanded news cameras be allowed to tour the prison. They wanted the world to see where they lived.

On a number of occasions, the governor chose to leave the gatehouse and speak to the public: the numbers grew by the minute. Journalists from as far away as Canada had descended onto the scene. Noting that his press secretary was out of town, the attorney general describes the first of King's interactions with the public:

> Reporters said later that questions from family and friends of inmates often ended the sessions. The information most sought after by journalists and families alike was, "Who is dead?" and "How many?" The status of the hostages was also a question of the press and public. But officials did not have names or numbers throughout Saturday to release. Rumors that as many as eighty had been killed were not effectively squelched for days after the prison had been resecured. Little consistent information was gleaned from the official briefings. Consequently, reporters tried to stop and interview anyone leaving the reservation. One ambulance attendant said the crowd at the road seriously hampered evacuation of the wounded.

Around 9:30 that Saturday morning, inmates offered their first official list of demands:

1. Reduce overcrowding
2. Comply with all court orders
3. No charges to be filed against inmates
4. Due process in classification procedures
5. Ten gas masks
6. Two new walkie-talkies

Only the fifth demand was agreed to.

That afternoon, as the killings in Cellblock Four reached their apex, more National Guard squads showed up. This time, they brought a medevac helicopter. The helicopter whipped up dirt and snow and caused panic inside the institution, with some of the escaping inmates rushing back inside. Ultimately, a helipad was cleared out far beyond the prison's boundaries.

The attorney general's report marks from 7:00 a.m. to 5:15 p.m. on February 2 as a time when many inmates, fearful for their lives, began finding their way out of the prison and toward the safety of the yard. Their methods were many and required equal parts ingenuity and dumb luck. For instance, the wrench Joe Madrid passed into E-1 at the beginning of the riot proved to save the lives of inmates inside that dormitory, who used the tool to knock out windowpanes and escape. Another group of inmates stole one of the cutting torches and cut through one of the construction grates inside the unfinished Cellblock Five. "Inmates continued to break out of the prison through any open holes not guarded by rioting inmates," the attorney general stated. "They came out singly and in groups, often fighting other inmates to escape."

Countless inmates spoke of the gauntlets one had to face in order to reach safety. After the riot, one inmate from Cellblock One, the honors unit, described having heard that the B-1 inmates had managed to break through the glass with Joe Madrid's wrench. He quickly made his way to the dorm to escape, but "[hostile inmates] weren't letting us go and they were blocking a thing in B-1. They had a hole there, [and] some goon squads or something was blocking it and not letting no one go out." A Black inmate described the desires and troubles of Black inmates trying to leave the institution. He claimed that, as he aided a blind inmate through Cellblock Two, where a hole had been cut: "They had . . . these two dudes that'd been there [a while]. They were there, you know, and they was killing dudes; and the dudes from Cellblock Two would drag [the dead] down to the gym; and, from the gym, they would drag them in there and throw them in that fire."

Those guarding the exits believed that the fewer inmates inside the institution, the less bargaining power the whole of the population had. In a cruel turn, the inmates themselves were now mirroring the actions of the administrators and guards following the notorious Thanksgiving food strike. Worse, those fortunate enough to make it to the yard unscathed and uninjured did not find safety at all. The riot was not over yet, and the inmates who'd opted out in a desperate desire for the aid of the state's judicial infrastructure were finding that they were being turned away from the fences. An inmate who found himself free from the chaos desperately tried to tell the police to act. "They asked me what's going on in there. I just told them, 'Hey, man, there's some people getting killed in there.' And they said, 'Yeah, we know.'" The Guard supplied escaped inmates with heavy wool blankets. But the inmates, who had gone without potable water for nearly twenty-four hours, only had cans of Vienna sausages handed out to them. "They didn't care," a former CO told me, referring to state officials. "To them, those guys weren't worth shit."

The yard was not without violence. The attorney general noted a number of instances:

> On Sunday just before noon, a large group of Hispanic inmates started to chase a group of Blacks in the yard and shout "kill the Blacks." The Blacks stopped at the perimeter fence near the sally port where they were ordered by law enforcement officers to drop to the ground. A Santa Fe County sheriff's deputy, Leopoldo Gurule, ordered a group of twenty National Guardsmen and law enforcement officers to "lock and load," and they leveled their weapons at the onrushing group of Hispanic inmates. At this, the Hispanics were given five minutes within which to retreat or be fired upon. Superintendent of Correctional Security Manuel Koroneos attempted to intervene physically between the officers and the inmates. Deputy Sheriff Gurule told Koroneos to remove himself from the range of fire or suffer the consequences. He moved. With just seconds remaining on the deadline imposed by Deputy Sheriff Gurule, the deputy ordered the group to aim their weapons. The group of would-be assailants retreated. The fence was then cut to isolate the Blacks in the area between the two fences.

Rapes were common, with one inmate telling the State Police he was raped by eighteen separate inmates while in the yard. Other inmates witnessed other sexual assaults. One told State Police: "They had a guy they call Despanada. They had him sucking everybody's dick in the yard. They had him inside that room where you get baseball equipment and stuff. They took a lot of guys out of Cellblock Four, and were fucking them."

■ ■ ■

Around 3:30 that afternoon, the inmates had settled on a list of demands:
Inmates' Demands and Officials' Answers

 1. Bring federal officials to the penitentiary to assure inmates no retaliation will occur.
    Answer: We will ask for the assistance of the FBI.
 2. Reclassify the men held in Cellblock Three. (The cellblock is used

to segregate prisoners considered to be a threat to the general population or those who may be the target of other inmates.)
Answer: Security risks will remain in Cellblock Three.
3. Leave all inmates in the units they were originally assigned to until the uprising is over.
Answer: We cannot agree to this until the prison's condition is determined.
4. End overcrowding at the prison.
Answer: About 288 beds will be ready in July and we have asked for an additional 200 from the legislature.
5. Improve visiting conditions at the prison.
Answer: This has been in effect for two weeks as worked out with the American Civil Liberties Union's negotiating committee.
6. Improve prison food.
Answer: We will hire a nutritionist to oversee the food operation.
7. Allow the news media into the prison.
Answer: Not until all the hostages are released.
8. Improve recreational facilities.
Answer: We are now negotiating with the American Civil Liberties Union.
9. Improve the prison's educational facilities.
Answer: This is being discussed with the legislature, raising inmate wages from the present twenty-five cents per hour.
10. Appoint a different disciplinary committee.
Answer: We will take a long, hard look at that.
11. End overall harassment.
Answer: We will have additional correctional officers who will be trained. The Corrections Commission is also looking at this problem.

Inmates were still adamant that the media be involved, that journalists were to hear their side of the story. Finally, ten hours after being promised a media presence, inmates Donald Stout and Michael Price met with both Ernie Mills and TV reporter John Andrews, just below Tower One, in the yard. The inmates laid out their grievances, and Mills listened. Ultimately, the inmates wanted to prove how bad the situation was: they demanded for a television news camera to enter the prison. Mills told them he could arrange for such the next morning. In response, the inmates released

Lieutenant Anaya. Anaya managed to walk himself to the gate, but by then his knees buckled and he collapsed. He was rushed to St. Vincent Hospital.

The negotiation worked, so far as prison officials were concerned. The process was repeated again at 10:45 that night, with the same inmates meeting the same journalists. The same demands and promises. Officer Juan Bustos was released.

But before long inmates felt taken advantage of. To quell this, officials decided to offer negotiators what they wanted: at midnight, Michael Shugrue, a cameraman for KOB-TV in Albuquerque, braved the walk from the yard to the administration building. He went alone, the only man on the planet inside the penitentiary voluntarily. If the matter were to be lost on him, it could not have been for long. One of the first images to meet Shugrue was the headless body of Paulina Paul.

For forty minutes, Shugrue filmed the ruined corridor, filled with blood and sewage. He filmed the heavy smoke emanating from the gymnasium. Shugrue later told an interviewer he had to stop filming at one point; his hands shook so much he could not focus the lens. But the NBC worker had a convoy of twenty-five inmates protecting him. They spoke to him of harassment and overcrowding. They spoke of lousy visitation rights, which could be taken from you at any moment. Some wore masks; others didn't bother, fully offering their names. In the background, noise came over the walkie-talkies. "Be careful," he told the attorney general's office. "Take somebody that's armed and ready to fight . . . there are two groups in there that are going wild."

As Shugrue left around 1:00 a.m. Sunday, inmates released Michael Schmitt. Officer Schmitt left the penitentiary on a cot puddling his own blood. He was on his stomach, his body bloodied and assaulted. Despite the blood loss, he remained conscious throughout his suffering.

■ ■ ■

Around 8:00 on Sunday morning, Officer Victor Gallegos managed to escape. He was not alone. Within the hour, the National Guard reported to the gatehouse that they counted roughly eight hundred inmates now outside of the prison. At night individual convicts used the darkness to escape, while at the break of dawn groups of twenty to fifty rushed the doors.

By noon, negotiators saw the release of Captain Roybal and Officer Ortega, with Officer Ronnie Martinez escaping as well. There were now only two hostages remaining.

At that same time, Ernie Mills was making good on his promise. He and a cameraman named Rick Johnson prepared to reenter the facility and give inmates their time on-air.

Prisoner representatives included Lonnie and Kendrick Duran (not related) and Vincent Candelaria. They met Mills and Rick Johnson in the visitation room. Lonnie Duran had a college background and read from a short statement. All three men had glassed-over eyes. Once the statement was read, the men extemporized on their feelings about the prison.

Lonnie's green eyes peeked out from beneath a beanie. "What's wrong with this institution is that there is too many Indians and not enough chiefs."

Candelaria, deep-voiced and mustachioed, chuckled. "You mean too many chiefs and not enough Indians."

Lonnie looked at him slowly, stoned and confused. "Well, all right. Too many chiefs and not enough Indians. That's what I mean."

The men ate powdered doughnuts brought to them by Mills. Kendrick Duran sat on the far end of the table, looking somnambulant.

"Each captain has his own set of rules," Lonnie continued, accidentally dropping his half-eaten doughnut. "At one time it was run by a captain and it run smooth. Now? There's a six-month waiting list to see the psychiatrists. There's guys in there walking around like zombies. They've got them on Thorazine or whatever it is. They don't belong in a penitentiary. They belong in a mental institution."

Kendrick Duran managed long enough to discuss the lack of incentive programs. Candelaria told the press he'd been beaten by correctional officers during the food strike of 1976 and that he feared it would happen again if inmates handed over hostages.

"That's our only play right now," Kendrick added.

The meeting shifted from the visitation room to the yard. Mills told the inmates they could speak directly to Felix Rodriguez. The group was soon joined on camera by Michael Colby and William Jack Stephens.

That Sunday was sunny but cold. The storm pattern had moved west, into the panhandle of Texas, and the air in Santa Fe was dry with a temperature around forty and rising. Ernie Mills reinterviewed Lonnie Duran and Vincent Candelaria, who reiterated their points—Lonnie this time accurately offering the chiefs and Indians aphorism. Candelaria told the media: "One of our questions is retaliation. Once we release the hostages, are they going to beat us?" He also stated that inmates needed to be transferred. Mills invited Felix Rodriguez onto the screen. Rodriguez told Candelaria, "You have my word: nobody will be beaten, shotten up, or anything else."

After this, Mills interviewed Michael Colby. Colby appeared with his aviators on, red mustache and red hair billowing out from beneath his beanie.

According to Colby: "What I'd like to say about this institution: the administration in this institution have been in here for over twenty years. Most of them are just a clique. They do anything they want concerning Cellblock Three. Dr. Marc Orner? Has threatened myself and Mr. Stephens, there, on several occasions. We were charged with escape, and it was because of [Orner]. They have threatened our lives. And they will continue to threaten our lives after we leave this penitentiary. The five of us are in jeopardy right now. No matter what they say, as soon as you leave, they're going to beat us and beat us bad. People may not believe that shit goes on, but it does. I've seen it. It's happened to me. They think we've done wrong? This penitentiary is twenty years behind any joint in the United States. I think that can be proven by records. I think what we've done here is right."

Jack Stephens, a black eye developing, a blue bandanna around his neck, wore a dark green sweatshirt beneath a navy prison-issued coat. "I was housed in segregation about three and a half months ago for attempted escape," he told Mills. "The reason for that escape was I was being threatened by inmate staff—Dr. Marc Orner, in particular. People were telling me every day that Marc Orner had a grievance against us and was not going to allow us out of the penitentiary alive. I feel as long as I'm in this penitentiary I'll never get out alive."

(It was alleged by both Anglo inmates and in the October 1994 issue of *Prison Life* that Orner would treat criminals by placing them in full-body casts with ports for urination and feed inmates pills, a suggestion Orner has adamantly denied.)

At this point, Colby interrupted the proceedings to tell Stephens and Mills that Felix Rodriguez had guaranteed the transfer of the five negotiators, to begin on February 4—the next day. Colby forced Rodriguez to make the guarantee again, this time on camera. Rodriguez acquiesced, with the understanding that the final two hostages were to be released first. At 1:26 p.m., both Officers Gutierrez and Larry Mendoza were released. The riot was over. Soon, the National Guard formed lines and marched into the prison. The act was largely symbolic: still fearing an Attica, Governor King had ordered, unbeknownst to the guards, that the rifles be loaded with blanks.

■ ■ ■

Carlos Martinez's unit was the first to tour the damage. "Everything was smoking," he told me. "Anytime I smell a burning building, I remember that afternoon." They were asked to subdue any inmates still among the ruins. "There were some that were so messed up they didn't know what they were doing. They weren't violent. You'd get one that would try to kick and fall down. So we'd handcuff them, take them out. Handcuff them, take them out."

Martinez's unit remained on-site until Wednesday, February 6. The prisoners had gone for nearly forty hours without sleep, and now it was Martinez and his men's turn. In the hallucinatory deprivation that followed, Martinez was not sure what was real and what wasn't. That was normal in the days after the pen had been retaken. The sights inside were otherworldly. The gymnasium had been destroyed by fire, as had the warden's office. People passing through the central corridor were ankle-deep in water, sewage, and blood. The Protestant chapel had been ransacked and then burned. The Catholic chapel remained remarkably pristine.

To make matters worse, the Guard had prepared for armed conflict. Instead, they learned now of their new assignment: morgue detail. Accompanying officials narrated the backstories to the bodies they found. Horrors such as Junior Urioste's and Paulina Paul's. What kind of justice system allowed these things to occur? While many law enforcement authorities and government representatives blamed the prisoners—"They're not human," state senator C. B. Trujillo was overheard muttering as he left the facility after the tour—Martinez immediately saw the trouble as lying within the system itself. Perhaps those former friends who mocked him for joining the Guard ("They called us Mickey Mouse soldiers," he told me. "We weren't trusted.") had been right all along.

As his unit bagged and carried bodies, Martinez caught a name he recognized. Nick Coca, who had succumbed to smoke inhalation in the officers' mess hall.

Nick was his first cousin, the son of his mother's sister. "I knew he was from Taos, and that we were related," Carlos told me, "but I'd never really met him." Carlos continued: "Nick was a screwup, a small-time burglar and drug addict. He'd steal things from people's houses to sell for drug money and get caught and locked up, then set free, and start all over. Most of his life was spent in the system."

Once they had Coca's body in a coroner's van, Martinez remembered the rest of the story. Late on an autumn night three years earlier, Nick Coca had dragged a woman from her home into the wilderness near Taos and repeatedly raped and beat her with a pipe. The attack lasted nearly twelve hours. The victim managed to escape and find a hospital. During the arraignment a month later, Coca snuck a razor blade from his jail cell inside his uniform and repeatedly slashed his right arm. Blood sprayed across the courtroom. Finally, a year later, Coca was sentenced: life plus 262 years.

Outside the pen, officials scrambled to figure out what to do with the thousands of inmates still alive. Inmates who'd surrendered and required medical treatment were transferred to St. Vincent Hospital in Santa Fe, to the Presbyterian Hospital in Albuquerque, and to the Santa Fe Indian Hospital. The 717th and 744th National Guard Medical Detachment provided evacuation by helicopter and ambulance. Uninjured prisoners were taken to the Santa Fe County jail, the annex, and to State Police District Headquarters to be privately interviewed.

None of this was conducted with anything resembling organization. As brutal as the chaos of the riot was, the postriot actions were downright incompetent. The first buses of inmates left the smoldering carcass of Old Main on February 6, with prisoners heading in every direction of the state, to every county in the state and beyond: inmates were flown to facilities in Arizona, Leavenworth, and Oklahoma. One hundred and fifteen inmates were flown to Illinois and redistributed throughout the federal system. Writers for the *New Mexican* witnessed these first buses pull away from Old Main and were shocked by the system being used by corrections. Supervisor Felix Rodriguez could produce for the press only a Stone Age tracking system: "Asked afterward by department aides how many men had been transferred to federal custody . . . Felix Rodriguez shocked onlookers by pulling from his pocket a soiled matchbook cover on which he had recorded the number."

Bruce King made it clear that under his administration the Penitentiary of New Mexico was already moving in the right direction. By February 7, three hundred inmates had been chosen not to be relocated but to remain at the facility. The following day, they were back inside and in charge of cleaning.

On that same day, February 8, Carlos drove back up to Taos. He'd hardly slept in five days but didn't relish the opportunity. Anytime he closed his eyes he saw the faces of the dead. He went first to his father's house for a cup of coffee before returning to his trailer for a shower. Carlos saw a letter in his father's mail from the Corrections Department. They regretted to inform Mr. Martinez that his son had been killed in the riot. "I thought it was just another screw-up," Carlos said. "I wasn't killed. I asked Dad about it, but he waved it off, too. He said, 'You know how crazy things are down there.'" This was a plausible story. Misinformation was running unbridled.

While Carlos rested and followed the story of the riot in the papers, he noticed that his father was taking the matter especially hard. All of New Mexico was in shock and mourning, given New Mexico's relatively small population: nearly everybody in New Mexico knew an inmate or guard inside. As case in point, there is the now infamous story involving state senator Manny Aragon, a rising star within the Democratic Party, who arrived outside of the prison on the evening of February 3, and Lonnie Duran. Aragon was there as part of the governor's envoy, but soon he spotted Duran in the yard, during negotiations. The two had played softball together as youngsters and had remained friends throughout childhood. As smoke poured out of the institution, Aragon and Duran began to ask each other how their parents were doing. But sometimes Carlos found his father quietly weeping and trying to conceal his tears. Carlos reasoned that the false death report had spooked the old man.

Finally, one afternoon Carlos walked over to his father's house. He told the older man he was going to talk to the state department about the death notice. What if they cut off his social security? What if he couldn't join the police academy? He joked that the police probably wouldn't want to train a dead man. He asked for the notice so that he could take it to the proper offices. His father didn't laugh. He refused to look at his son.

Through tears, his father told him the truth: as well as his first cousin, Nick Coca was Carlos's half brother. He admitted to a longtime affair with Carlos's mother's sister. Carlos sat back in the chair and considered this. He had always prided himself on taking the moral high ground. He was willing to take the verbal abuse from Taos residents because he felt, to a large extent, a rectitude that would manifest itself in time. That morning he learned his half brother was Taos' most notorious criminal. He'd carried his own brother's body out of the smoking prison. The days after the riot shook his sense of what shape his career would take. Now he had another identity crisis to deal with—one that went to the core of his familial life. For a young man who believed in the virtue of truth, the winter of 1980 was unveiling to Carlos that the world around him was filled with lies.

PART THREE

CHAPTER EIGHT

Gary Dru Williams managed to escape the gauntlets uninjured and make it to the yard. He found himself in the mass. He tried to find his brother, but there was a careful dance to this. The threat of savagery still remained. To ask another inmate about Jeff's whereabouts could find Gary labeled as a snitch. Conversely, Gary ran the risk of asking the same clique who'd attacked Jeff about Jeff's condition, thus placing Gary as a witness to what had occurred. There existed many perils. The roaming rape squads, the hysteria of racial violence, and the medevac: somebody in the throng announced its intentions to firebomb the campus; another said they spotted a machine gunner dangling above its landing skids. From the Madrid Highway, the shrieks of families. From the pen, cries for mercy. The press and its klieg lights; the police and their red-and-blues.

Ultimately, it didn't matter. Before Gary could find any information about his brother, transit vans pulled onto the grounds. Fearing lawsuits, the corrections department began a mass parole of seventy low-classified inmates as a sort of psychological reparation. Gary was among them. His time as a custodian of the New Mexico Corrections Department had lasted less than seventy-two hours. He was back in Carlsbad before all victims of the riot had been identified. By February 11, Judge Edward Snead suspended Gary's bond and the sixty-day diagnostic requirement. Some sixty days later, he'd be given probation. He paid $1,000 in fines and was released into the custody of his parents.

∎∎∎

On February 4, 1980, the *Carlsbad Current-Argus*'s headline read, "Prison Death Toll Rises to 35." The *Argus* quoted Governor King as saying that around fifty inmates were unaccounted for. In fact, three weeks after the riot, authorities were forced to admit that they could not verify the location of more than 120 inmates.

The discrepancies were enough to cause chaos, but adding to it was the lack of a consistent, official narrative. Governor Bruce King and his office would offer the papers an account of the missing and the dead, only to be undercut by a far different number from Warden Jerry Griffin and corrections. State Police officials had their own number of dead and missing, which was incompatible with either.

Even small details led to disagreements between officials. Governor King was quick to point to overdoses as a cause for 20 percent or so of the deaths. Almost simultaneously, the Office of the Medical Investigator told a different news outlet they were certain none of the dead had succumbed to overdoses.

All departments were clear on one issue: no inmate had escaped. Those missing were simply a matter of paperwork. "If I'm doing fifty years and I can take the ID off a guy doing five," the governor said, "well, that sounds like a good deal."

Jeffrey Lloyd Williams was not among the missing, at least not initially. Beginning on February 4, Dubb and LaDon and Gary followed Jeff's name among the critically injured. His name first appeared in the *Current-Argus*. Beneath the large headline claiming the death toll, at the bottom of the first page, a short article gave these details.

A local radio station, KBAD, said it had been informed that Jeff Williams, Carlsbad, listed as in serious condition, was one of those injured. Reports to the station said Williams had been transferred to an Albuquerque hospital. He reportedly had his right hand almost severed during the uprising. Doctors had sewn the hand back on, according to reports, and he reportedly also had been beaten about his head.

The news was grim, but better than the alternative. Unfortunately, the Williams family, along with most of the families of victims, had no recourse—no manner in which to glean more details. The hospital switchboards were bombarded, and, in an effort to not add to the chaos, families were barred from entering the hospitals. The state was offering daily—often retracted or revised—names of the survivors. The information was so maddening that by the time news of Jeff reached the Williamses, a near-violent clash had erupted between the National Guard and families holding vigil outside of the prison. The families, around one hundred deep and frustrated with the lack of information, approached the prison from the front gate, demanding answers. They were met by Guardsmen and police armed with

M16 rifles. The authorities physically shoved this group back down the road, beyond the front gate. The crowd was largely comprised of mothers and wives of prisoners.

On February 5, as state officials still struggled to provide answers for family members of men housed at the penitentiary, the Soviet Union released an international statement, calling the riot a "bloodbath." The state news agency TASS told its readers: "Riots in the US . . . are an inevitable consequence of the anti-humane character of the US Corrective System . . . US authorities use any pretext to do away with imprisoned opponents of the existing order and quite often resort to physical extermination of prisoners."

On February 6, the *Argus* reported that Jeff had been transferred to Presbyterian Hospital in Albuquerque, where, "it was said that Jeff Williams . . . is still in serious condition. The hospital would not give details on his injuries or where he is located in the hospital."

On February 7, his name appeared in the *Albuquerque Journal*, listed as one of four inmates still hospitalized due to the seriousness of their injuries.

On February 8, his name was listed again at Presbyterian in Albuquerque—this time as having gone from "critical" to "improved."

After February 8, no journalist, hospital staff member, or corrections department administrator could say where Jeffrey Lloyd Williams was.

CHAPTER NINE

Throughout the rest of that spring, an inertia came over the Williamses. Less than sixty days after Gary had come home, the afternoons in Carlsbad were averaging around 70 degrees, with sunny and cloudless skies. People were taking their boats out onto the Pecos River for the first of the season's waterskiing trips. Gary now lived in his old bedroom, with a mother who could not stop crying and a father who spent his days on the telephone, demanding answers from anybody who would listen. Gary had no job and nowhere to go.

As the weeks dragged on in the spring of 1980, Gary felt as though his chest would burst from his rib cage; he contemplated anything, everything. Having seen Joe Madrid's beaten and stabbed corpse just outside Jeff's dorm, seeing inmate Ray Vallejos and Officer Mike Hernandez beaten through their pleas for mercy. He understood the world now as a place where people could commit the most heinous of brutalities onto the weak, and laugh while doing so.

His brother was still unaccounted for.

What had Gary gained? He had less now than he had before he moved to Toledo. His mother, a Baptist, was spending an awful lot of time with psychics and witchy people. Dubb was largely silent, or at the Elks Club on the hill overlooking the Pecos River, drinking. He told Gary he was happy to have his son back, but it was evident that Jeff's absence weighed far heavier on Dubb's mind than the return of his eldest.

That summer, one of the nation's deadliest heat waves settled in over the mid- and southern plains. Temperatures in northern New Mexico topped out at 100 for four weeks. In July and August, Carlsbad was averaging 104.

As for the riot, the state had settled on a final body count of thirty-three. Kelly Johnson was the last victim to be identified. It took officials more than a month to confirm his identity—such was the state of his body.

During the first week of June 1980, Attorney General Jeff Bingaman published the official narrative, *Report of the Attorney General on the February 2 and 3, 1980 Riot at the Penitentiary of New Mexico: PART I*. In late July, inmates who'd been transferred out of state began to return to Old Main. By August 8, 1980, the State Board of Finance added nearly $230,000 to the district attorney's office, giving the state prosecution $700,000 to work with. Grand juries were sworn in. Assault, homicide, and rape charges had been handed down. In other words, authorities were ready to put the ordeal past them. They had accounted for everything. They had their narrative.

And then, one month later, in September, something truly bizarre happened. After months of speculation, months having not been accounted for by any New Mexican authority, Jeffrey Lloyd Williams suddenly appeared, materialized, on national television.

CHAPTER TEN

Two hundred and thirty-three days had passed since the Riot at Old Main. Two hundred and twenty-eight days since Jeff Williams had been reported on or discussed by any journalist or state official. And now, on the night of September 23, 1980, he appeared on ABC's national broadcast *Closeup*, a precursor to *Dateline*. The episode, entitled "Death in a Southwest Prison," began with a broad overview in Tom Jarriel's southern drawl. His voice-over carried throughout the setup.

Eleven minutes and five seconds in, Jeffrey Lloyd Williams appeared on the screen. Donning a wide-brimmed straw cowboy hat pulled down to his eyes and a leather jacket, he sat before the bare wall of a motel room. He had scars on his cheeks and nose. He hadn't shaved in some time, but his youth was still evident, found in the uneven way his mustache sat beneath his nose. Williams told *Closeup* what happened to him in the smoky corridor where he'd gotten lost:

> We were walking toward the front [entrance] and I got a little bit sep-
> arated and I bumped into somebody in the smoke and the next thing
> I know I'm getting stuck. Boom. Stuck here and there. Steel rods are
> coming down on me. And I see a meat cleaver come in. I stuck up
> my hand and that cleaver cut right though the bone and everything,
> and my hand just went over. I went halfway down, and was getting
> stuck and beat on. It took three or four hundred stitches to sew up
> my head.

Gruesome photos of the cicatrices on his wrist and scalp were shown. The photos made clear somebody wanted Jeff Williams dead.

An associate producer on the *Closeup* documentary told me filming occurred around May of 1980—at least two months after the riot and after the attorney general's task force had concluded their official findings (Jeff's name appears nowhere in the account). As stated, after February 8, no media outlet mentions Jeff or his whereabouts either, save for one.

The ABC news piece, coupled with Felix Rodriguez's matchbook count during the riot, led to a special, five-page exposé entitled "Barbed Wire" published by the *Santa Fe New Mexican* in early 1981. The investigative team for "Barbed Wire" was comprised of reporters from two newspapers, a television station, and Albuquerque's public radio station. The project took nearly a year to complete and was perhaps New Mexico's largest journalistic undertaking: relying on internal memoranda and anonymous sources the report asserts that over the course of the year following the riot, staff officials "have been involved, directly or indirectly, in the murder and attempted murder of inmates, brutal beatings of inmates, a black market in contraband inside the prison walls and the misuse, personal exploitation or outright theft of prison funds." The "Barbed Wire" investigation also argued that "no one knows with certainty how many more inmates may have died or vanished" beyond the official count. Jeff is used as a primary example. In October 1980, they wrote: "Inmate Jeff Williams, mortally injured in the riot and as a result quietly paroled to St. Vincent Hospital on Feb. 11 . . . died of his riot wounds in a Las Cruces hospital. Williams was the 34th but unannounced victim of the riot."

The state had decided on a death count of thirty-three; this was reiterated in the attorney general's report. As far as escapes, the official line, claimed by the governor, the warden and deputy warden, the secretary of corrections, and the attorney general's office was that no inmate had escaped.

The details within "Death in a Southwest Prison" and, later, "Barbed Wire" shocked the citizenry. If nothing else, his appearance on ABC proved that the state was simply wrong about there having been a full accounting of inmates postriot. If this was true, they could be wrong about a lot of things. But the allegation of there being a thirty-fourth death—and perhaps even more—caused widespread astonishment. Before Jeff's appearance, the governor had promised the most sweeping reform to prison function in American history, and the attorney general's office had promised its narrative would be the most comprehensive investigation possible, one that would lead to "lasting solutions." House Bill 275, adamantly supported and signed by Governor King, had allotted over $38 million in taxpayer money to rebuild the prison. In one appearance, Jeff had undermined the state's credibility.

The production of "Death in a Southwest Prison" had not been an easy undertaking. Writing a preview of the show for the New Mexican citizenry, Dave Nordstrand told readers of the *Albuquerque Tribune* that the hour-long focus was jinxed, offered nothing new about the narrative, and suffered from tunnel vision. Nonetheless, Nordstrand was quick to point out the difficulty with which ABC found working with the state's corrections department. Only one month earlier, a piece had aired about New Mexico's uranium policy, and Governor Bruce King had come off as derisible. "King won't be happy about his second involvement with *Closeup*. . . . The Federal Bureau of Prisons gave ABC the go-ahead to enter the federal prisons where New Mexico inmates were being held, but then changed its mind after an appeal by New Mexico officials. . . . After repeated efforts, including an unsuccessful trip to federal court, *Closeup* finally got its day in the pen. 'But that was on Aug. 28, after most of the show was put together,' [Stephen] Fleischman, producer, said. Fleischman says King and Rodriguez had assured him access to the pen, but when the ABC crew arrived to film the project, they found access blocked."

Once it'd aired, the *Tribune* wrote a follow-up, calling the documentary worthwhile, and opining on the origins of the riot. "Although the show presented nothing that New Mexico hasn't heard; the show put the focus of the State Penitentiary's problems back where it should be—on the people of the state and their indifference to the corrections systems . . . ultimately, the blame was laid to rest at the feet of New Mexicans. We are the ones who must demand changes in the administration of the penitentiary."

Corrections' responses to the media were, post-ABC, summed up when Systems Warden Joe Gutierrez claimed the entire exposé was "a damn lie from the word go." The battle continued: officials called journalists liars and underminers, while journalists made claims based on sometimes-capricious sources. The state would then, once again, deny any validity to these claims.

Jeff Williams had spent his life basking in the outlaw lore he'd created around Eddy and Chaves Counties. But in his appearance on *Closeup*, Jeff speaks softly, his eyes darting around whatever saturnine motel in whatever shit town where the interview was filmed. Even then it must have appeared to viewers that, as Williams responded to questions, he began to realize what a mistake it was to be on television. The rest of the show focused on the general riot; Jeff added nothing to this narrative—he was there simply to show his scars. No other injured inmate was willing to appear. Only three other prisoners were interviewed. One in deep shadow. And Michael Colby and William Jack Stephens.

Finally, the authorities reported to the *New Mexican*:

The corrections department refuted a report that inmate Jeff Williams, mortally injured in the riot, died of his riot wounds in a Las Cruces hospital. The corrections department said Wednesday documents show Williams actually died in Mexico and was a parole absconder at the time of his death.

Less than a month after *Closeup* debuted, the Williams family received a call. Corrections told them what they would later that day tell the press: "The body was returned to the US, where it was identified by authorities."

■ ■ ■

The body of Jeffrey Lloyd Williams was found in a pecan orchard in the agricultural town of Ciudad Delicias, eight hours south of Carlsbad. His obituary declares a date of death as October 14, 1980, though this is spurious. A coroner in Mexico determined the cause of death as being "a cerebral embolism" while another coroner listed "*shock as brought upon by gastrointestinal bleeding*." His obituary claims Williams died of a heart attack. The autopsy report, mailed to the United States before the delivery of the body and verbally translated from Spanish to English, was read to Jeff's parents. Exhausted, dumbstruck, and traumatized, Dubb and LaDon signed the report and had Jeff's body transported to Carlsbad. Jeff was twenty-four years old.

West Funeral Home, in Carlsbad, hired an ambulance to drive to the border and retrieve the body. (West Funeral Home was owned by the Garretts, LaDon's family.) The driver had been a young man whom I later spoke to with the assurance that I would not disclose his identity. There were rumors I'd heard since childhood that something had happened during the ambulance drive—a stop in the middle of nowhere followed with some Houdini, body-double stuff. The driver laughed and assured me this was not the case. He did tell me that Jeff did not look like a heart attack victim. His death did not seem natural. The driver refused to elaborate, admitting that it would be entirely circumstantial.

Once back at West, the family and a number of officials came together. What they saw was shocking. Jeff looked so much older than twenty-four.

His head had been shaved; there were scars all over his body. Television had not done justice to his injuries. Tom Cherryhomes found himself at West Funeral late that evening. I'd mentioned that Jeff's ambulance driver had intonated that something unnatural had occurred. Cherryhomes did not hold back. "Jeff had a bullet hole in the back of his skull. He'd been shot and tied to a tree to die alone."

If the autopsy results were meant to close the discussion on Jeff—if they were meant to end questions about his absence for corrections—it only created a new series of more complex questions. Why had corrections listed Jeff Williams as a parole absconder when Jeff had never been granted parole? Was it at all possible that Jeff, as wounded as the evidence now proved, managed to regain his strength, hop out of a hospital bed, leave the building unnoticed, spend eight months on the lam crisscrossing New Mexico and avoiding criminal justice, only to be found by ABC at a motel with ease? And, of course, the big question: Who killed him, and why?

On a more intimate level, viewing *Closeup* served as a trigger for Gary Williams. Seeing Jeff one last time led him to believe that his family had been lied to. How could he not feel that way? All they had been told, countless times, had been lies; the television appearance proved as much. So, Gary reasoned, which narrative now made more sense: that a twenty-four year-old died of a heart attack, or that, given his brother's potential as a witness and victim of an attempted murder—his own attempted murder—Jeff had used the *Closeup* special to expose his case (in this context, the interview feels like a plea for help, a man coming as close as he ever will to testifying against his attackers) before making his way to Mexico in order to avoid retaliation, only to run out of room?

Gary knew something had happened, and that he would never get an accurate narrative from officials. Later that autumn, he sought answers.

CHAPTER ELEVEN

Immediately following the riot the New Mexico State Police began interviewing survivors in the annex building of the penitentiary. These interviews lasted for more than a year. Some began as soon as February 4, before inmates had had a chance to overcome sleep deprivation. Primarily, investigators were interested in homicides. When narcotics trafficking was believed to be involved in the violence, agents from the narcotics investigation team were brought in. This was the case with (among many others) Michael Colby, Darrell Stelly, and William Jack Stephens. They were among the first to be interviewed, with Stelly interviewed on multiple occasions.

Convicts with long rap sheets are as wise to interrogations as those doing the interrogating. To read the interviews with Colby and Stephens is to read a master class in dissembling. Yet there are moments when the inmates gave away information that looks, in hindsight, to be crucial.

Stephens wanted to emphasize to police the fear, not furor, that Anglos felt during the riot. An agent, whose name is being kept anonymous, asked Two Pack directly about death squads. Stephens said he only knew of them "because I was down in B-1 at one time and they was all barricaded in, you know. And four or five of my partners was in there, and I told them, 'Yeah, well, come on man, let's try to make it to the front.' They said, 'No, we're going to stay in here because there's a death squad out there killing white folks.'" While this anecdote is meant as an alibi, it instead places Stephens as a member of the crowd outside of B-1, Jeff's dormitory, coaxing those inside to step beyond their ramparts.

For his part, Michael Colby admitted to being in every location within the institution but swore he never stepped foot inside Cellblock Four. He offered insouciance toward the killings.

> AGENT: Hey, would you say that they opened all the cells and let everybody out and they let the wrong ones out? I mean, they were out to kill and stuff? Just started killing everybody? Is that what caused it or was it the dope or . . .
> COLBY: I think a lot of it was grudge killing and then the snitch killing. Killing them old rats and stuff. I understand there were

several killed in Cellblock Four, which is the protection unit. That's understandable, I guess.

(Years later, speaking to the BBC, Colby had changed his narrative: "Were you in Cellblock Four?" they asked. "I've been in Cellblock Four before, yeah," Colby responded.)

He also claimed to the New Mexico State Police that he did not hear any screaming during the riot, saw no physical acts of violence, witnessed no rapes, and knew of only one acetylene torch, given to "inmate negotiators" directly by Secretary of Corrections Felix Rodriguez to cut holes in the institution so that inmates could flee the building.

Darrell Stelly, who had escaped with Michael Colby and William Jack Stephens in December 1979, claimed to have spent the thirty-six hours in an overdosed state.

But dozens of eyewitnesses, many unknown to each other and housed in different units, told the New Mexico State Police that the Anglo squad had armed themselves with equipment stolen from the kitchen. Their weapons were described with alarming uniformity.

A Cellblock Four inmate named David Fuentes offered the following to the State Police: "[Colby] was carrying that chrome machetetype knife. I guess it was about two foot long. He had been sniffing or taking drugs. And "Two Pack" was with him. He had that spade, that big old spoon, looked like a spade, aluminum, that come out of the kitchen."

Another inmate told police: "Michael Colby, that's his name. He came down the run with a carving knife in his hand, about eighteen inches long."

Others offered the following:

A little bit later on the redheaded guy, he just got on a murder charge out there, wears glasses. Michael Colby, that's his name; he came down the run with what looked to me like a carving knife in his hand about eighteen inches long, and went on the run . . .

■■■

They opened the doors and went on in. And inmates started walking up and down the tiers with night sticks, clubs. This big Black dude had a white riot helmet on, banging at the doors. And then Michael

Colby came down. He had a big, looked like a, one of the bread knife–type knives . . . and he was banging on the bars telling people to get their blocks out of their doors.

■ ■ ■

Colby hit him with that big knife-type thing, and you can just see his head fall back.

■ ■ ■

And Tex stabbed the Black guy, but he didn't kill him, so Colby says, "I'll show you how it's done!" And he took that huge knife and he slashed the Black guy's throat or whatever he did. He tried to cut his head off. They thought it was a big joke.

■ ■ ■

Q: And you recognized Michael Colby?
A: Yes, sir. He was carrying that chrome machete-type knife. It was, I guess it was about three foot long.

■ ■ ■

When Michael Colby turned around at that time, he was carrying this knife. Must have, it's, I guess, estimated its length around, uh, two feet. And it was pretty wide. It was a machete-looking object. It was sharp and chrome-plated and it had a black handle.

■ ■ ■

One of them, a redheaded dude, Colby, there you go, he come up there and he's red and his eyes are just like the color of that [un-known] there. He had, looked like a machete or something like that, in his hand. Silver-looking thing, from the kitchen.

■■■

Q: Did Colby have anything in his hand?
A: Yeah. He had one of them big old mop handles and, a, this fucking machete-looking thing.

■■■

When Colby walked by my cell with that big fucking cleaver, I cowered. I'm terrified of that guy.

■■■

Colby went downstairs. He had this cleaver. He said, "You mean you all can't kill this punk?" He said, "I'll show you how to kill this punk. Get his head. Pull him up here." The cleaver swung and pulled back, you know. He said, "That's how you kill a punk," and walked away.

■■■

Investigators were adamant that the Anglo clique had used the chaos to solve debts. They believed Jeff Williams likely to have been a failed hit during the riot. New Mexico State Police agents asked Stelly about this when inquiring about which riot deaths Colby had been involved with.

AGENT: Did he mention who?
STELLY: He didn't mention any names.
AGENT: Well, he must have said some names, Darrell. Uh . . . ?
STELLY: None. You know, he just went . . . the thing with Mike Colby is that he just got burnt on that other killing. And he's still real paranoid about that. And he doesn't talk about, about the crimes at all. He hasn't given me any specifics whatsoever.
AGENT: Did they mention who did the number on Jeff Williams?
STELLY: No.
AGENT: Do you know?
STELLY: No. I don't even know who Jeff Williams is.

CHAPTER TWELVE

"If you really want to know Gary Williams," a friend of his told me, "just look at his luck. He's promised this arson scheme would be easy money. Instead, he's arrested. First day in prison? The riot. He comes home. Nobody cares. Everybody's saying, 'Where's Jeff? What happened to Jeff?'"

The focus on Jeff didn't dissipate with the finding of his remains. The lawns along Riverside Drive were pockmarked with REAGAN-BUSH BRINGING AMERICA BACK signs, but citizens of Carlsbad found themselves equally drawn toward the salacious. It would be difficult to blame them. Without clear accounting from the state, the citizens were left to fill in the narrative.

The narrative from Santa Fe had not changed. By the time Jeff had aired on television, the first allotment of the $38 million emergency prison budget had been used to renovate the interior. The walls had been repainted, and an updated control center now stood at the destructive knot of the corridor's halfway point. The National Guard was in charge of meals, and most inmates said the food had changed for the better. Santa Fe District Attorney Eloy Martinez told the public to expect between 75 and 125 charges for felonious actions undertaken during the riot. Given the amount of time and the undertaking this would require, Deputy District Attorney Richard Baker said that priority would go toward death penalty cases. The optimism from the DA's office was in line with the state's.

But inside the pen, the blackened outlines of torched bodies remained. Dozens of axe marks scarred the concrete of the gangways. And the district attorney's confidence belied an incredible reality. In exchange for shortened sentences, many inmates agreed to serve as witnesses for the state. Any opportunity for lesser time is attractive to inmates, but just as had been the case with Bert Duane Stevens, the responsibility falls to the state to protect the witness. New Mexico hadn't learned its lesson. Many of these cases dragged on for two years, and New Mexico still only had one maximum security prison. Accusers were housed in the same facility as the accused—the same facility that had been destroyed over the course of thirty-six hours. The number of prisoners now pleading to join protective custody dramatically rose.

This included former hardcore inmate Moises "Troca" Sandoval. Sandoval was the first to be tried in a riot murder, that of Leo Tenorio—the inmate whose neck had been snapped by a radiator cap after being thrown from the third tier to the basement. Troca opted to help the state in other cases and, after a number of stabbing attempts against him, did not return to the general population until 1985. That year, he asked to be allowed back onto the main line. Five hours later, he was killed. Jose Jesus Antunez, facing the death penalty for his involvement in Ramon Madrid's horrific burning, was tried next. He was stabbed to death before the trial had completed.

These are two examples of the twenty-four deaths and twelve violent attacks that took place between 1980 and 1982 at the penitentiary. The riot killers were now being killed. The effect on the district attorney's office and their cases was devastating. Even they could agree: this was not a reformed institution.

"No shit," Marcella Armijo told me and chuckled. It was funny in retrospect but difficult to live through. Some of the penitentiary's new problems were directly impacting Armijo. A new warden, Robert Tansy, held a meeting early into his tenure. He told the officers, "I want to be real straightforward. I'm not going to have a female running the day shift."

Marcella said, "The other COs were looking at me to see how I'd react. I said to Tansy, 'What did you say?' And he said, 'I told you. I'm not going to have a female running the dayshift.' He told me it wasn't personal. Well, I was the only fucking female." Armijo filed a lawsuit.

In the interim, she watched with disgust as corrections hired new officers, promising them safety that did not exist. Five new guards were hired. They were called a "new order" of officer. None of them had direct ties to higher-ups, and all of them went through far more rigorous training. They'd come in earnest, told that they were there to prove New Mexico was on the right path. "We were hired to be something of reformers," one of these new order guards, Mahlon Perkins, told me. "We were there to stomp out any corruption." Marcella was placed as their unofficial captain. Many were startled by her cynicism, which was at odds with the classroom lectures they'd heard.

Only four months into this new order, Officer Louis Jewett Jr. was stabbed while breaking up an inmate fight. He died four weeks later. A few months afterward, Officer Gerald Magee was stabbed to death by three inmates—all of whom were known to have participated in the more brutal goings-on of the riot, and all of whom were eventually exonerated for killing Magee after an evidentiary bag went missing. At this point, the new order no longer felt, if they ever had, that the state was behind them. All five resigned by 1981.

During those years, Armijo worked even longer hours to prove the new warden wrong. When those long hours ended, Armijo would not go home to her husband and daughter; instead she went to the bar with her colleagues. At the bar, she tried to keep pace with her fellow guards, many of whom had one hundred pounds of body weight on her and were alcoholics—a common condition among correctional officers nationwide. "I was hitting the bottle hard, just with the guys. You should've seen me, man. I went through hell. Not knowing what was happening to me. That was the scary part. Not only me. It took a toll on my whole family. On my one daughter, poor thing."

Her husband left. He won sole custody of their daughter. At the same time, Marcella's overtime at PNM was noted, and soon Armijo was promoted to full captain. She was the first woman in American history to have done so. It was the height of her career. It was also the most miserable point in her life.

Things were proving no better for Marc Orner. Following Jeff Williams's appearance on TV, prison administration decided to no longer cooperate with the media. The psychologist, however, broke from this policy. The memo he'd written warning administration that a takeover was imminent was leaked to the *Albuquerque Tribune.* Its contents were validated by a letter written by an inmate named Randy Pense to his wife Donna. The letter arrived at the *Tribune* bureau a day after the Orner memo. In it, Pense told Donna that administration "knew it was going to happen but took no steps to prevent it."

The joint publication of these documents led to an ugly battle between administration and the counselor, which also played out in the media—though abstrusely. Corrections hired Dr. George Solomon, a "California specialist" on prison relations. Solomon conducted an investigation paid for by the state; its findings placed blame for the riot on "distrust of therapists, and rape." Solomon's judgments have never been regarded as worth entering the general discourse about the riot. His conclusion reads as a hatchet job. Solomon mentioned Dr. Marc Orner by name. "Particularly on the issue of confidentiality, Dr. Marc Orner, the . . . psychological services director, was singled out by inmates as being involved in the security functions of the institution to the detriment of the treatment functions of his position."

Very quickly, Orner found himself the scapegoat for what'd occurred at Old Main. He wasn't a man to take such an accusation without responding. Orner fired back at his employers and worked with the *New Mexican* on an article about financial fraud. "Orner told team investigators of hidden and suspect discrepancies of several thousands of dollars in the current pen pharmacy accounts, as well as in the budget of the institution's psychological unit."

In response, the corrections department fired him. They didn't stop there. An unnamed official within the department alleged to the FBI a gun-running and drug-smuggling operation based at Aspen House, a rehabilitation center overseen by a group of therapists for whom Orner served as director. "The memo cites reports that cocaine and heroin from Colombia to Albuquerque to Miami and Los Angeles is dealt at Aspen House." If this weren't enough, the allegations included far more gruesome details. Also cited was the story of one of Aspen House's tenants raping his wife with a hot curling iron. A formal investigation was undertaken into the matter, and while Orner was never charged with any misdoings, his career, his reputation, and his personal life in New Mexico were left in ruins. The state had torn him apart.

The postriot milieu, in other words, was as violent and opaque as it had ever been. It reached beyond prison walls. Soon all state citizens watched with dismay as the district attorney's office lost case after case.

CHAPTER THIRTEEN

A 1983 memorandum written by attorney Mark Donatelli to the District Public Defenders and Riot-Private Council within the Public Defender Department begins by noting that the district attorney's office had planned for "up to 75 capital indictments." As an outcome of the defense work, Donatelli notes that "no defendant-inmates will serve any significant additional time as a result of the riot and . . . no death sentences were imposed."

Despite a war chest nearly three times that of the public defender's office; despite having to battle their own chief public defender, who placed a gag order on all defense attorneys, thus letting the DA's office use the press without rebuttal; despite the average prosecutor billing $75 an hour to the public defender's $20, the outcome for the state was nothing short of a rout against their favor. Thirty-one cases against twenty-one publicly defended inmates resulted in two guilty verdicts. Thirteen of the cases were dismissed, eleven ended in plea deals, and five in acquittals. As Donatelli points out, "Of these clients who received [plea deals] perhaps three may have their parole dates delayed 2–3 years because of riot sentences. . . . Thus, little if any additional time will be served by any of our clients as a result of the riot prosecutions." Regardless of private or public defense, no inmate received a death penalty for crimes committed during the riot. On the other hand, and to rub salt into the wound—and prove the further cruelty of the still-alive snitch system—Donatelli's memo points to inmates who opted to serve as prosecutorial witnesses rather than take their own defense. Of the six given as examples, the first received: "3 lifes [sic] concurrent with each other . . . "; the second received "30 years consecutive to his present indeterminate sentences"; the third, "6 year[s] consecutive to present sentence"; the fourth, "9 concurrent and 9 consecutive to present indeterminate life" (this inmate was Black); the fifth, "8 years concurrent with a 7-year sentence"; and the sixth, "9 concurrent with a life sentence that is consecutive to his present sentence."

They were all, in every sense, death penalties.

Mark Donatelli was a young attorney from Purdue University with a thick mop of tight curls and a laid-back manner that contrasted with his inexorable commitment to defensive counsel. Not only did public defenders work tirelessly for Donatelli and for little money, but they also found resources in out-of-state defense council. Basic and early strategy came from attorneys who'd been present at Attica and Reidsville, at the Wounded Knee Occupation of 1973, and others who had experience with large-scale litigation cases. Donatelli thanks these efforts; he also thanks the Southern Poverty Law Center and the NAACP Legal Defense Fund, but his biggest praise is for an attorney from Oklahoma named Garvin Isaacs.

■ ■ ■

If Canyon Road has come to exemplify the arts in Santa Fe, it was Harry Georgeade's Bull Ring that exemplified its political culture. The steakhouse was inside a two-century-old adobe dwelling next door to the capitol building. Former senator Sander Rue told the *Albuquerque Times*, "You always wondered who [was] going to be there. There were legislators, lobbyists, cabinet secretaries. You go there to network, bump into people. During my day, a lot of the committees would have their annual dinners there. It's very much a part of the history of New Mexico state government."

On a warm June night in 1982 after all court proceedings had closed, Garvin Isaacs found himself at the Bull Ring bar, which was known for its excellent pours: boulevardiers and rebujitos. Garvin stuck to Coors.

He had two reasons for drinking that night. The most immediate was basketball. June 3 marked Game Four of the NBA Finals that year. Isaacs, a fan of the game, was hoping to watch Magic Johnson and the Lakers capitalize on their 2–1 series lead over Dr. J and the 76ers. The game was on at the bar.

The second reason—the one he wished to escape for the night—was far more dire. Garvin Isaacs, a well-dressed Oklahoman with a tight mustache and a commanding, down-home drawl, had not had New Mexico prisoners on his mind before Mark Donatelli alerted him to the problems inmates were facing. Isaacs respected Donatelli's mind as a defense lawyer. Before long, Isaacs found himself on a flight to Albuquerque and, in the morning, standing with Donatelli in the tiny living room of Mildred Colby's house in the Nob Hill neighborhood.

"She was like the mom in *Any Which Way but Loose*," Garvin Isaacs told me. "Just absolutely ruthless and devoted to her child."

Michael Colby had been implicated in the torture and death of Larry "Grandpa" Smith, along with Richard Buzbee, James Humiston, and Richard Nave Chapman. Colby was facing capital punishment. Garvin Isaacs had agreed to assist the public defender's office in the case, but all at once Mildred Colby was adamant he serve as lead counsel. She remortgaged her house to afford Isaac's services.

For Isaacs, it was a losing case. Before the riot, Michael Colby had made a reputation for himself in New Mexico—first, with the baseball bat murder, and then all over again mere months beforehand, with the December escape. Now he was facing capital murder, and the newspapers and local news affiliates had run photographs and B-roll of him endlessly since the riot. Beyond the court of public opinion, there were dozens of fellow inmates' testimonies.

Isaacs remained hopeful. The state relied on three witnesses: James Humiston, James Kilker, and Gregory Raklios. Humiston had pled guilty to the murder of Larry Smith as soon as charges were placed upon him, Michael Colby, Richard Buzbee, and Richard Nave Chapman. Isaacs not only pointed to this as a factor in Humiston's testimony; he also mentioned a "mysterious visitor" to the Española jail, housed in a small town north of Santa Fe, after which these inmate eyewitnesses decided to come forward and name Michael Colby as the assailant. (I've been unable to find any information about this Española visitation, but Isaacs's brilliance was to lean into a narrative an already-gobsmacked public would not find preposterous.) Isaacs was quick to dismiss James Kilker's testimony. Kilker was known to be as close to Larry Smith as a brother. Under cross-examination, Kilker admitted that he only saw a redheaded man outside of Larry Smith's cell—not a face. And he admitted that he hadn't considered Colby until the name had been brought up by the district attorney, eight months before the trial. "Most folks' memory of an event blurs as time passes," Isaacs told the jury. "Mister Kilker's seems to sharpen." As for a third state witness, Greg Raklios, Isaacs pointed out that he had already been paroled and was living on the other side of the country, doing "just fine."

As the trial neared its close, Isaacs left the courthouse for the Bull Ring, feeling assured of his work.

Game Four of the Series was held at the Forum (now known as the Kia Forum) in Los Angeles. The game was being broadcast on CBS, and at halftime, the voices of Brent Musburger and Bill Russell gave way to

KGGM-TV in Albuquerque, the state's principal news outlet. The bar filled with patrons, swarming for refills and to settle tabs. Anchorman Bill Yeager's voice interrupted the prattling.

Isaacs couldn't recall the exact words, but he said, "[Yeager] came on during halftime analysis. 'We interrupt this report: Michael Colby, now the most feared outlaw in New Mexico since Billy the Kid, awaits his fate in the notorious torching and murder . . .'"

Isaacs didn't stick around to hear the rest. "I thought, 'Oh, my god. We're done.' I was so bummed out. I never felt so bad."

The problem was that the jury had not been sequestered by the judge. They'd been free to go home before deliberating. Isaacs pictured how many of them had just heard Michael Colby compared to Billy the Kid. "I couldn't sleep," Isaacs said. "I was just going nuts, so I decided to do something." In the morning, a Friday, Isaacs asked the judge to voir dire the jury. "Denied. I moved for a mistrial. Denied."

Isaacs said he haunted the courthouse that weekend, hardly sleeping, trying as best he could to sway Judge Tony Scarborough for any leniency. Finally, on the morning of Tuesday, June 8, Isaacs found himself hanging around the east doors of the municipal building, red-eyed and delirious. The sun was just beginning to rise when a custodian, somebody Isaacs had befriended during his late days and nights at the courthouse, walked up to him. "He walked up to me, looked around, saw that the hall was empty, and said, 'You got nothing to worry about. They acquitted Colby on the first ballot. I know because I dumped the wastebasket out.'"

It turned out to be true. Isaacs had planted enough doubt in the jurors' minds to see Michael Dennis Colby exonerated. Members of Colby's family cheered. His mother, Mildred, went to kiss him but was denied. Instead, Colby turned to the courtroom audience and grinned. He raised his hands high, fists pumping, before bailiffs handcuffed him and escorted him back to the penitentiary. Neither Colby nor his close friend, William Jack Stephens, would be found guilty of any crime during the riot.

CHAPTER FOURTEEN

Gary did not last long enough to see the Colby trial end. But even as the autumn of 1980 finally ended the historical hot streak in the weather, such scenes were common. Gary, like every New Mexican, was aware that the state was failing to convict anybody accused of violence during the riot. As attorney Mark Donatelli's 1983 memo points out, nearly all defendants were exonerated. The moratorium placed on media interviews by the chief public defender might have inadvertently helped defense cases. As the prosecutorial offices, the governor, and the new administration at the penitentiary spoke with orotund machismo, the quiet results of the defense amounted to a collective discombobulation.

"Gary didn't know what to do," Cherryhomes recalled to me, "but he knew Jeff was into drugs. He started there. He had always been deliberate, conflict-avoiding, shy. But after Jeff died, he started hanging around druggies. He was deeply interested in the drug trade, which runs from El Paso, through Carlsbad, and up into both Albuquerque and Santa Fe."

Cherryhomes thought perhaps Gary wanted to emulate his deceased brother, but he reasoned it was far more likely that Williams had decided on a foolish escapade: to be his own undercover private investigator.

By Halloween 1980, Gary had grown so close to a man named Garry Heffner that he accepted a gift: a 30-06 shell casing hiding a tiny cocaine spoon. Gary Williams wore it as a necklace. Heffner offered something even more valuable: a concrete place to find people who knew the truth about his brother's fate.

Not much can be found about Garry Heffner. Citing a desire to move forward and to remain positive, his ex-wife kindly refused to speak. What is known is that by 1980, his drinking and cocaine abuse had led to the divorce and to Heffner drifting through the southern badlands. He had family in Carlsbad and, after a few stints in county lockups, attained a tenuous connection with this newfound Aryan Brotherhood.

On Thanksgiving Day 1980, Gary Williams rented a Monte Carlo—the same make and model Jeff owned. He, Heffner, and a third man, whom authorities have never publicly identified, began a trip up Highway 285 from Carlsbad to Santa Fe. Sometime around midnight, the rented car met a blizzard. The men pushed on, making it thirty miles north of Roswell, near Poverty Flats Ranch.

Before daybreak, south of Vaughn, Garry Heffner found a payphone and called the police. He told them that he needed help. He said he had been riding in a car when Gary Williams opened the door and let himself out. He could not see him in the rearview. It was too dark. He had no idea where his passenger had gone, or why he'd ejected himself. When police arrived, they did not find the third, unnamed accomplice. Only Garry Heffner remained, along with the Monte Carlo.

Heffner was allowed to go back to Carlsbad of his own volition. He was never charged, nor was he named a suspect by the Chaves County police. Without a body, they figured, they could not substantiate any claim of a disappearance.

Nonetheless, the sheriff's office began aerial searches using a helicopter. Dubb paid a friend to do private searches in a Cessna. A week passed without any sign of Gary. LaDon consulted the psychics she'd been seeing since Jeff's death. Her most trusted told LaDon her boy was in a "confined deserted area, possibly an empty service station."

The search continued throughout the year.

As 1980 ended, Dubb and LaDon Williams had no clear account of what'd happened to either of their two sons.

■ ■ ■

"New Mexico is fifty years behind the rest of the country," an attorney, who wished to remain anonymous, told me. "And the conditions inside law enforcement were fifty years behind that. You're talking 1880. People go missing. The cops don't see that as strange."

New Mexico is the prettiest state in the country. It lacks a beach. It lacks a Rodeo Drive. Santa Fe, the toniest town the state has on offer, is brimming with bizarre characters. "The City Different" is its motto. Some citizens wear raccoon hats to Walgreens. Every day is Halloween, a Baptist preacher once told my family. It is sometimes also cheekily referred to by residents as the Land of Entrapment—a take on the state's motto, the Land of Enchantment. The land is more important than any creature dwelling upon it. A shithouse can run for $2 million—not because of its accoutrements but because of the geography. To go missing in New Mexico is standard fare: the land can and will dissolve you. And those in charge do not find this notion remarkable. "People go missing." Maybe there is something to this. It has always been the land that has mattered, far more than its people. This was Spain's initial entry into North America, and the venture spilled more blood than we can account for. The land mattered.

When Charles Martin found a body on his property on New Year's Day 1985, he'd assumed it was that of an itinerant worker. "Happens a lot," he told me. "Some desperate folks traveling on the road get lost, and it is vast out here, and there ain't exactly landmarks to follow." He tended to share the general feelings others raised about missing persons. It was a surprise to see the caravan of law enforcement vehicles arrive at Poverty Flats that morning. "There was excitement about it for them. It lasted a while. When they left with the body, a detective said he'd be in touch with me. I never heard back."

Charles Martin did not know Gary's identity until I told him. He did not know that Williams had been present during the riot. This was not an accident—or perhaps it was a simple by-product of local and state authorities. The autopsy had listed his death as a homicide. He'd suffered blunt force trauma to each knee, though hypothermia was listed as the likely culprit. By the time he had been identified—by the time his obituary ran in the *Current-Argus* on January 10, 1985—the case had shifted from the hands of Roswell's detectives to those who worked for the New Mexico State Police. From there, it disappeared. The detectives assigned to the case have passed away, and the actual case files have since gone missing. The only possible reason given for this has been vague discussion of it being damaged in floodwater and discarded.

How easy the shift had been from sending multiple units to Poverty Ranch to forgetting the case altogether. Garry Heffner was not investigated by police. As far as the unidentifiable third man—the one who was also missing from Vaughn by the time Heffner had called police—it appears authorities never investigated who he might have been.

■ ■ ■

Decades have passed, yet I found many New Mexico state employees were still disinterested in talking about anything connected to February 1, 1980. After receiving a grant from the National Endowment for the Arts, I spent time back in Santa Fe to collect stories from anybody who would speak. Naively, I thought the task would take three or four months. It took more than four years. Everybody might have had a story, but a willingness to share their stories with an outsider proved another matter entirely. Though the riot has now marked its forty-fifth anniversary, many are still afraid of retaliation either from government officials or from former convicts now freed. Almost immediately upon returning to Santa Fe, I ran into taciturnity. I found myself again and again stood up for interviews or talking only to voicemail.

One day, I parked myself at the State Records and Archives Center. I'd been corresponding with a senior archivist via email for months. She had been tremendously helpful; she'd put together a finding aid of more than four thousand documents. I arrived at the center with hundreds of dollars in quarters, put on a pair of white gloves, and began photocopying this invaluable cache.

Two hundred pages in, the archives bureau chief returned from lunch. She asked her senior archivist who I was and what I was copying. Then she put down her lunch and walked over to the photocopier, took what I'd copied from the tray, and tore the pages apart. "You can't have these," she told me. "They're off-limits."

The attorney general's office got involved. Finally, days later, the bureau chief met me in her private office. She said she would grant me access to the archived material but warned it was stupid to pursue them. "I don't think you understand how things work here," she said. I began to tell her that I was born at St. Vincent's but before I could finish, she interrupted me: "There are families here who don't want this information out. You'd be smart to go back [to] wherever you're from and forget about this. Your life might depend on it."

I'd never been threatened by a librarian before.

The threats, warnings, and obfuscation continued for two more years. I'd call a court clerk's office in, say, Farmington, with a case number and then drive hours to the courthouse, only to find that particular file suddenly missing or injudiciously redacted. Microfiche terminals did not work. The copier lacked toner, or paper. Asking for names of detectives working on cases led to obituaries. Freedom of Information Act (FOIA) requests took months and often ended with an email stating that there was nothing there to send my way.

I managed, finally, to reach a New Mexico State Police officer on Facebook. He was a homicide detective who met with the Anglos alongside another officer—one interested in the drug trade behind bars. We didn't converse so much as I floated questions his way and he ignored them. Instead the agent spoke in an interrupted monologue. The details he felt needed to be made public did not necessarily correspond to my questions—and he was more than happy with that. In fact, only once did the agent directly respond to a message:

Jeff went to the prison after he escaped Chaves County jail in Nov. 1978. By March, he had Stephens and Colby down as defense witnesses for his trial in early April, 1979. Of course, the PNM had to big escape that December—was Stella involved with that, or Price?. There is the theory that Jeff put Colby and Stephens on the Chaves County defense witness list so that they would be moved to Chaves County in late March / April 1979, at which point they could more easily escape, according to Jeff, than the PNM.

Of course, the other theory is simpler: Jeff was a Demerol addict, and by the time of March, 1979, he thought he was friends with people who were not his friends. He didn't go to trial in April, 1979—he elected to swallow a razorblade and then, later, pled guilty. So this other theory puts forth the Jeff was attacked during the riot (but didn't die) because he owed debts.

Do either of these sound reasonable?

A tiny heart, the only reaction I ever received from him. He was not willing to elaborate and soon went quiet.

■ ■ ■

Days after my correspondence with this agent ended, I happened upon the contact information for a person as close to having an answer as I have come.

I am not a journalist. My formal training is in fiction, with a background that prepared me to imagine lives and worlds rather than to dissect them. I have lost countless nights to the questions that preoccupy those who tell stories about real lives: the ethics of naming witnesses and victims, the repercussions of exposing those accused but acquitted, and the boundaries of what can be shared on-background or off-record. These are not simple questions. This story is not mine to resolve, and yet I have watched it go unresolved by those tasked with seeking the truth. But I've come to understand the power of silence, and that silence can be its own ethical failure. In such light, I have chosen to quote directly from an email shared with me by this source. It is a decision I have wrestled with. Withholding it—leaving this voice unheard—feels complicit in a system that has avoided asking the hard questions. Sometimes the only ethical choice is to continually ask certain questions aloud, even when the answer feels impossibly out of reach.

I asked this person about the relationship between Colby, Two Pack, and Jeff Williams—specifically, about their Colby and Two Pack appearing on Jeff's defense witness list in Chaves County. After a brief discussion, I was sent the following:

> I'm quite convinced that [escaping Chaves County] was it. Upon reading your note mentioning your guy's attempted escape it became clear to me. Prisoners were always immediately aware of new guys and their charges . . . once Mike and Jack learned he was to go back to trial they would have immediately told him to list them. Probably the Chavez [sic] County jail was already well known.

Jeffrey Lloyd Williams, a Demerol addict with a severe debt owed to those who ran the drug trade behind bars, had, likely, traded as the only way to pay the debt, a ride to Roswell, a jail known at the time for its ease of escape. Panicking, Williams swallowed a razor blade in order to serve his time at the far less violent mental hospital in Las Vegas, New Mexico; however, he found himself back at Old Main. He likely asked for semi-protection and authorities saw him fit for life inside B-1 and was housed there when the December escape happened and then failed.

OLD MAN GLOOM

On the Friday before Labor Day in 2016, I found myself standing in the outfield of the sandlot at Fort Marcy Park on the north end of Santa Fe. On a hill not terribly far away stood a fifty-foot marionette with red lips and bat-like ears and angry, deep-set eyes. In a few hours, the puppet would come to life, its arms pointing angrily at the crowd, its jaw moving as a voice groaned, cackled, and tormented those below. Finally, its personage would be set ablaze.

I went there to meet Sonny Hezemans.

Actually, I went there to write about the Burning of Zozobra for a magazine. I'd booked tickets to be in the city during Fiestas de Santa Fe and was ready for a feature article, but a xenophobic fearmonger working for Glenn Beck's *The Blaze* beat me to it. (Later *The Blaze* posted a video of the construction of the marionette and its burning on YouTube, claiming it was a citywide form of satanic ritualization. The video has since been deleted.) I was hoping to salvage the trip by speaking with Sonny, a man who'd been a maintenance supervisor at Old Main in the year or so after the riot, and a man whom I knew only by way of a few strange phone conversations.

The Fiestas de Santa Fe is an annual civic happening held early each autumn. It is a celebration of the day in 1682 when Don Diego de Vargas led conquistadores back into town and recaptured it from Pueblo Indians in a "bloodless and peaceful" manner. Each of the three dominant ethnic groups handle some aspect of the celebration. Those of Spanish descent begin the Fiestas with a Mass at St. Francis of Assisi Cathedral. The Mass ends with a procession in which La Conquistadora, a twenty-nine-inch wooden figure of the Madonna and Child, is removed from the cathedral and taken to the Rosario Chapel and Cemetery. Throughout the week, the Pueblo tribes hold an open-air market of jewelry, pottery, leather goods, and paintings. They host formal dance and music exhibitions and offer traditional food items for sale in the town's plaza. The fifty-foot marionette is known as Zozobra, or Old Man Gloom. It is a custom to burn him either at the conclusion of Fiestas or at its beginning. A month or so before Fiestas, Gloom Boxes appear outside of the newspaper bureau and at various civic buildings. Santa Feans drop into the boxes things they wish to say goodbye to in the new year: divorce papers and tax liens, a lot of cancer diagnoses and foreclosure agreements and final notices. One year, a woman turned in a blue hospital gown; another year, a man turned in an acoustic guitar for reasons unknown. These are in turn shredded and make their way into the guts of Old Man Gloom.

Despite *The Blaze*'s attempt at clickbait, the tradition is not at all satanic. *Zozobra* is a Navajo term, but the practice isn't ancient or Indigenous. His contribution to Fiestas is from the Anglo community and began in 1926. The product of a local artist named Will Shuster, Zozobra and his burning quickly became the climactic moment of the event. When Shuster died, the rights to the marionette were passed on to the Kiwanis Club. Proceeds from the event go to local schools and to park development projects.

In 2016, event planners calculated the attendance around fifty thousand, with tourists from around the world. Here on this day in early September, Santa Feans show up to burn the worst of their pasts and turn that burning into beautification. I thought Zozobra would be the perfect place for Sonny and me to meet because Sonny had a lot of past to burn.

Before becoming a traveling salesman for an agricultural company with specific expertise in pivot irrigation systems, Sonny had been in-country during Vietnam, came home addicted to opiates, lived on the streets of Albuquerque as a heroin addict, kicked the habit, found religion, and spent fourteen months as a maintenance supervisor at Old Main. He was a member of a team in charge of the "new" prison, its grates and general maintenance, meant to restore the reputation of the New Mexico Corrections Department. It became clear to him fairly early on that one of the job responsibilities not mentioned by authorities was an ability to witness incredible violence while fixing, say, the plumbing system. After the stabbing death of correctional officer Gerald Magee, whom Sonny had grown close to, Mr. Hezemans said he could no longer stomach his job at the institution.

"I often tell people to this day that my experience on the ground in Vietnam?" he'd told me by phone. "It really occurred at that prison. It was so much worse. Every day I didn't think I'd walk out alive."

Fairly early into our correspondence, I knew I could not use Sonny Hezemans as a source. Although the timelines, organizational charts, and events with which he spoke matched to a tee the historical facts of the institution, there were times when, allowed to extrapolate, Sonny would veer the conversation toward the bizarre and even downright incredulous. He'd hint at alien abductions, vast global conspiracies, and the Second Coming. He alluded to things he could not talk about. He called the state government a "fifth column," though for what or for whom he never made clear.

(Similar to the obfuscation by authorities, these wild rumors were and are still common. In fact, in 2016, a former inmate named Samuel Chavez was given by the courts an allotted time to dig for documents he said he'd buried on the grounds that would prove the prison was involved in torture and that prisoners' "organs and blood were sold for profit." The dig found nothing, and four years later, Mr. Chavez was sent back to prison on an unrelated burglary and weapons charge.)

Nonetheless, I wanted to meet Sonny in person. I wanted to know his story. Even if it wasn't factually reliable, the pathos with which he spoke was compelling. By now, my home office in Texas was littered with facts: pink pages of architectural prints, mugshots, datelines, interviews, and autopsy photographs. I wanted to know how those involved with the institution felt about how their lives had come to unwind since.

I knew that Carlos Martinez, the National Guard member who had found the body of his half brother Nick Coca in the wreckage of the prison, had succeeded in his dream: four years after Old Main, he joined the State Police. He married, raised children of his own, and upon retiring found himself restless. He joined the DWI task force in Carlsbad. The program is officed in a squat stucco building adorned with an enormous mural that reads, DWI. The Price Is Too High. Broken Lives Shattered Dreams and is accompanied by an image of two wrecked cars on a lonesome highway, a dead body lying on the pavement while patrol officers look on, and what are either aliens beaming up to outer space in an aura of violet light or souls leaving the body—it's difficult to tell.

This is where my aunt Cindy Sharif works as program director of the DWI prevention team. Martinez is her right-hand man. When I spoke to him, I couldn't help but notice that underneath a consummate professionalism, there was raw emotion about the lie his father told him. He feigned not caring. "I asked my half sister about Nick," he told me. "She said we rode the bus together. I don't remember that." He told me nobody had a photograph of Coca. "It isn't surprising. He entered the system at eighteen." When I asked Carlos about the details of Nick's untimely death, he shrugged. "I've always just guessed he was a snitch."

Nick Coca was many things, but he was not a snitch. An interview with a law enforcement officer details as much in the February 7, 1980, issue of the *Taos News*. The article appeared the day after Coca's remains were positively identified. Coca, thirty when the riot occurred, was not the victim of the more salacious violence. He did not have a dramatic end. Rather, attempting to escape the fire that had begun in the case file room and spread to the gymnasium, Coca, in the dark of the smoke, cornered himself in the officers' mess hall. He succumbed to smoke inhalation.

I told Carlos Martinez this as delicately as I could. He listened to me, and when I was done, he shrugged, offering no other reaction to this news. Carlos saw this as many in law enforcement have: a direct consequence of criminal behavior. But the look in his eyes was the same as so many I'd interviewed. The riot. Speak these words in New Mexico, and everybody knows exactly what you mean. Everybody lost somebody. Everybody lost.

Sonny Hezemans, I felt, could contribute in his own way. He was born in a town in central New Mexico known for its beauty and for its mountain skiing. After he resigned from Old Main, he left the state and has never gone back for any significant time. During one of our phone conversations, he happened to mention traveling through northern New Mexico on a sales run. I invited him to meet me for the burning. "I love New Mexico," he told me. "It's beautiful. It's my home. I definitely left the state over [Old Main] and I'm never going back."

I likely knew even then that Sonny would not show. I knew that Marc Orner, like Hezemans, had left the state, vowing not to return. Orner may have once been drawn to the state's natural beauty, but this was not enough to keep him around. He left the same year Hezemans did, working in family counseling by day and by night coming home to a heavily secured and heavily armed household—such was his fear of retaliation forty years removed from Old Main.

When I invited Sonny to the Burning of Zozobra, I was trying not only to find information on the corrections department right after the riot but also, for some strange reason, to rectify this man's relationship with the past and with the state. In time, I was able to convince him to give me a soft verbal agreement to spend at least a few hours in New Mexico during the Labor Day weekend.

When the sun set over Fort Marcy Park, a light rain began. Some people had come with umbrellas. I hadn't. The rain made the grass of the outfield gummy on the soles of my shoes. But it did not deter the burning of Old Man Gloom. Around 9:00 p.m., his eyes suddenly turned to green lasers and his jaw flapped wildly as he shouted at us. He turned his head from left to right, waving his arms in condemnation, his left index finger pointing with judgment.

The burning is a catharsis, and demands a violent and public exhibition. In 2016, the fire first took hold of the monster's arms before spreading down the right flank. When the muslin gave way to the chicken wire of his fingers and hands, it was not long before his arms disintegrated into smoldering ash and floated above us. The inferno took some time to reach his head, but once it did, it spewed from his open jaw. He continued to groan, his anger now agony. A tip of flame came off his fedora and rose in a high point. The crowd was filled with young children, some of them holding Zozobra dolls, all of them cheering. Many of the adults were drunk. The air was pungent with pot. An old white man danced to a song his brain was DJing. Old Man Gloom was disappearing in front of us, though the groaning and crying would not stop until the fifty-foot structure finally fell forward, a clump of embers on the top of the hill.

Sonny did not show that night. I've not spoken to him since. I've heard he has lost his job as an agriculture salesman and is living in Minnesota somewhere, struggling once again with drug dependency. The idea of returning to Santa Fe was foolish on my part and could only have ended badly for him. I see now that what I wanted was a novelist's ending. The personification of the past, a public burning to mark catharsis and progress. The metaphor was so tidy.

The past isn't tidy. Not in a place haunted by where the holy faith lives in the air and the blood of the soil; where the soil itself at Chimayó, a tiny town in the mountains roughly an hour's drive north of the capital, can cure you of the most debilitating diseases. Where there are rumors of self-flagellating brotherhoods long since mistrustful of any papacy dictate prior to the Council of Constance in 1414. Where it isn't unusual for people simply to disappear. It isn't unusual for somebody to vanish and for law enforcement merely to shrug shoulders and comment that it happens more often than you think. There are ghosts. William Jack "Two Pack" Stephens died in Old Main's infirmary from HIV complications. Michael Price died of hepatitis—perhaps here or perhaps in Chicago, but certainly inside the hospital of a penal institution somewhere in this country. When Darrell Jean Stelly was transferred to California, he opted to rat on his Anglo brothers, believing he was safe after the transfer. To his horror, he found himself back at Old Main for a half year. Each month he placed $10 on Michael Colby's books—an effort both to apologize for running his mouth and to keep himself safe. There is no record of where, if anywhere, he is today.

Michael Colby, on the other hand, is a free man. In 1998, an attorney managed to win his freedom arguing that New Mexico had not accurately tallied his time spent.

But even the living seem haunted. The last time I saw Dubb Williams was on an early July day, at my grandfather's funeral. Dick Blenden gave a fifteen-minute eulogy, met with the funereal version of applause: nods of *thank you* and hushed affirmations. We went to the cemetery for the graveside memorial. I am certain the reverend gave us all some loving words, healing words. I couldn't focus. It was too hot and my shirt collar clung to my neck, and two seats in front of me, Dubb sat, listening. Thirty-four years had passed since the riot. Dubb was old but still held his hair, slicking it into a duck's ass. His outfit also included denim overalls, white athletic socks, and dusty, black penny loafers. Watching Dubb's tiny skull in front of me nod with the pastor as we lowered my grandfather's coffin, it was impossible not to notice how very close we were to his family's plot— to where his sons rested. *Oh me; there again,* Hecuba says in Euripides's tale of her loss. *Oh my children, thy miserable butchery!* It was difficult not to look at him and be reminded of the tale: Hecuba entrusts her son to Polymestor, who in turn kills the prince-child out of greed for the gold left with the boy. In retaliation, Polymester loses his children to a murderous and vengeful Hecuba.

What do we say about a man whose greed placed his children in the position of butchery? After twelve years of research, saying that there are no answers is maddeningly frustrating. It is gloomy. And yet it seems a condition this state has come to accept as natural.

I have tried to accept it, too. Watching the crowd of Santa Feans quite literally move through the act of catharsis left me with a tinge of regret that Sonny could not or would not join in. Yet in order to find catharsis, Sonny Hezemans would have to return to the one place he wished never to be again. Or perhaps Sonny has it right. Perhaps there's a larger irony at play. Maybe he understands that the people of Santa Fe find relief from gloom only to have to return to the ritual every year, the past never really burning, never turning to ash and disappearing into the night. Never really going anywhere.

EPILOGUE

Old Main continued to serve as the state's primary carceral institution until August 1998. It closed in disrepair. To the northeast, only perhaps five hundred yards away, lies a Level VI supermax. The previous facility was mostly forgotten until a decade and a half later, in 2012, when New Mexico began planning events to celebrate the state's centennial. Governor Susana Martinez called on all state agencies and local authorities to organize centennial events that would engage the public. Albuquerque held a concert—featuring everybody from the Bethlehem Baptist Church Steppin' for Christ praise dancers to Los Lobos—and fireworks display. The many museums of Santa Fe invited guests to presentations on the history of art in the Desert Southwest. The Department of Health staged a film and lecture series on one hundred years of Hispanic health improvements.

Corrections wasn't exempt from the directive, but its secretary, Gregg Marcantel, was at a loss. It is, in a fundamental sense, the department's job to keep its day-to-day goings-on independent from the public.

Eventually, Marcantel alighted on an idea. On occasion, the old penitentiary had been rented to Hollywood for $1,000 a day to shoot films, such as *All the Pretty Horses* and *Zero Dark Thirty*. But for the centennial, Marcantel thought the site could be better used to tell a different story—its own. He directed the department to organize tours of the facility centered on the history of the riot. Fifty-six years after Harold Swensen proudly opened Old Main's doors to reveal the state-of-the-art institution to the public, citizens were welcomed in once again, this time to tour its wreckage.

By the time the first tours took place in February 2012, state officials had come to recognize a version of events more in line with reality. The tours, which were invitation only, led people connected to the riot and interested in criminal justice through the derelict building where much of the original architecture and equipment remained. The walking tours followed no script, were guided by a varied and imprecise collection of people, and lasted three-plus hours. Attendees were asked to brave snow and ice, temperatures in the single digits, to forego bathroom breaks, food, and water, and to not close cell doors behind them as nobody had keys. Fallen tiles lay along the corridor. Every so often, a dead pigeon could be seen. In the basement, near the gas chamber, the air was of such quality that many visitors gasped and coughed, their eyes watering.

The tours were nonetheless a massive success. A total of two thousand people visited, and the New Mexico Corrections Department decided to expand them beyond the centennial celebration. When they posted $15 tickets on their website for the first Friday of every month, the tours sold out in days. They added Saturday. Those sold within weeks.

Officials saw potential, and in March 2013 they hired Alex Tomlin, a local television reporter, as public affairs director. They gave her the duty of moving the enterprise toward a legitimate museum-going experience. Tomlin was to write a script based on the attorney general's report that each guide could follow, and she began to brainstorm ways of making the experience unique. Secretary Gregg Marcantel also had ideas, which Tomlin could help implement—haircuts for tourists in the old barbershop and meals in the chow hall prepared by current inmates housed at the Level VI supermax.

Current inmates were awakened at the break of dawn and, wearing orange jumpsuits, mopped the old facility. When flooding occurred, these inmates were given push brooms. It became an important aspect of corrections to offer the public a unique experience. The new tours now ended in a gift shop, where visitors shelled out for goods handmade by men currently incarcerated. Once it was cleared of weeds and debris, the courtyard in the center of the facility was turned into a meditation garden—presumably with the labor of current prisoners. It was cheap labor for what some saw as an amusement park in its infancy. Respecting Our Past to Create a Better Future had been painted in the visitors center.

The corrections department held a special Survivors' Tour in October 2013 for former inmates and guards. "When we did the tour, I was kind of amazed at the difference in feeling, respect, and feedback," Alex Tomlin said. "Since then, we haven't had a single 'tear it down' comment."

Gary Nelson, who was locked up in Old Main on the night of the riot, was one of the former inmates to attend. "In a sense, seeing the prison did provide me a sense of relief," he told the *New York Times* after the tour. "It's over, you know? I'm never going back in there again."

Not everyone was happy with the direction corrections had taken with Old Main. One of its loudest critics was Marcella Armijo. When the corrections department wanted to award her a Medal of Honor for her long involvement in the industry, Armijo declined. "Now? A medal the size of a quarter? No, thank you. Fuck 'em," she said. She also passed on taking part in the Survivors' Tour. She had been honored in 1995 with the Trailblazer Award by the New Mexico Commission on the Status of Women. But by the time corrections had invited her to the Survivors' Tour, she began seeing these accolades as patronizing. "It's hard to accept what the prison is doing now. Maybe I'm real negative. I'm sure if I were to talk to Marcantel and all those guys they'd think I was a know-it-all," Armijo said. "I just don't want them to continue doing shit that is for [naught]."

After retiring in 1998, Marcella was diagnosed with PTSD. She viewed the tours in part as a glossy advertisement for the department, a tool by which they could cover up the incompetence that still plagued the state's penitentiaries. Armijo had been embroiled in a lawsuit with the state for decades, claiming that she and 179 fellow guards were never fully compensated. She also pointed to a lawsuit filed in February 2015 by five COs claiming sexual harassment and a violation of their civil rights. "My main point is that the state never helped us," she said. "It took a toll on my whole family. I went through hell."

■ ■ ■

On an unusually hot morning in July, I took a shuttle from the corrections department's central office parking lot to the drafty lobby of Old Main to take the tour. This would be my second time. Among the ten other tour-goers were a college-aged kid working on a report for summer school, a married couple with their mother, and two women from Durango, Colorado, wearing matching Louis Vuitton handbags. Though they didn't know much about the riot, the pair had read about the tour in a brochure at their hotel and thought it would be a fun thing to do. Upon arrival, we were guided to a desk behind glass where we were each assigned an inmate number and then led to a height chart taped to a door for a "booking" photo. A worker in a polo shirt embroidered with the words OLD MAIN AMBASSADOR attempted to allay one elderly woman in the group who looked particularly aghast. "It's just for fun," he said.

Most of the people tapped to be tour guides were reassigned correctional officers. Our guide, Cory, had worked on the line for four years before moving to a gang investigation unit. He walked backward as he led us down the main corridor toward the old control center. "I never turn my back on anyone inside an institution, not even civilians." In the control center, a plastic clock was permanently set to 2:02 a.m., the time it was destroyed by Danny Macias and the raiding E-2 inmates. Despite the presence of these clocks throughout the facility, the tour was almost Joycean in its nonlinearity, an outcome of Old Main's architecture and because whole areas of the institution were still off-limits. Visitors were forbidden from taking photographs in certain wings, including Cellblock Four, where the outline of James Perrin's scorched body was still visible. The silhouette of Jim Perrin's body had become, by then, something of a ghoulish memento of the riot. The legend told to spectators was that, despite best efforts, the burn in the concrete refused to ever go away. While tourists were no longer allowed to take photographs, this had become a relatively new policy; before that, the burned shadow appeared on cable TV ghost-hunting shows.

Tour guides had been encouraged not to shy away from the bureaucratic fuckups that led to the riot, drawing on information from the attorney general's report. But if a visitor lacked a working knowledge of the events, the meandering narrative would leave one with more questions than answers.

I'm not certain people tour Old Main for answers.

Coincidentally, two months after the prison reopened to visitors, the University of Central Lancashire launched the Institute for Dark Tourism Research. Academics have seen a trend in recent years. As Dr. Ericka M. Robb notes in her essay "Violence and Recreation: Vacationing in the Realm of Dark Tourism," we are no longer content to slather ourselves in Banana Boat and take in a few days of sun. We want an authentic experience; we want to know a foreign place by its "true" identity, and we assume, given media portrayals, that the best possible way to do as much is to have "a behind-the-scenes look at the daily lives of [usually] poor and disenfranchised hosts." Robb points to GlobalExchange.org, which, by way of example, allows interested parties to participate in "The Economic Justice Tour of Argentina." The organization states that such a tour, with a price tag of $2,690.25, will offer a unique experience:

> Inflation has skyrocketed, unemployment is spiking upward, debt continues to increase, and corruption persists. President Cristina Fernandez de Kirchner is facing mounting domestic criticism for

these and other related issues, and hundreds of thousands of Argentines took to the streets in September 2012 and April 2013 to protest. In light of all these issues it is a fascinating time to visit Argentina.

Professor Tony Seaton is noted as defining a new form of dark tourism, thanatourism, in which visitors "travel to a location wholly, or partially, motivated by the desire for actual or symbolic encounters with death, particularly, but not exclusively, violent death."

In the vein of Baudrillard, scholars of dark tourism are suggesting that media saturation has led us to the inevitable: the best holiday is that which allows us to experience death without dying. I saw this in the eyes of my fellow tour-goers. We weren't here for answers or for historical context. We were here because here, once, was death. And we were here, too, because it allowed us to experience a nightmare held in the American collective consciousness: prison. We know, by way of HBO series, network dramas, cable documentaries, and secondhand tales, that there is no worse place on our soil than a penitentiary. It is our stand-in for the leper colony of premodern Europe. Massive facades on the edges of towns, just off our interstates, barred-off and bleak. Their very presence, at least for me anyway, lends itself to a moment wherein the joy of a road trip pauses, replaced with a good long stare. For the price of a cheap lunch, Old Main offers us the experience of savagery while knowing soon enough we can retire to the La Fonda hotel bar for an afternoon margarita.

The afternoon before our tour, a rare thunderstorm had moved across the Sangre de Cristos and down onto the plains, and the Cellblock Four basement held pools of stagnant rainwater. After showing us the burn marks, the hatchet scars, the places where inmates were tossed from the top tier, Cory led us into the gallery near the control panel. There, we paused. He told us a success story from Corrections Industries, a branch of the department intent on offering current inmates opportunities to learn trades.

"When we said we were going to allow prisoners to bake cakes and to have access to baking utensils, people imagined a bloodbath," he said. "[Inmates] love it. We've never had a problem."

There was a lot of this banter, all of it optimistic. The slogan, "Respecting Our Past to Create a Better Future," is more a mission statement or a marching order—one every administrator, landscaper, or volunteer prisoner knows by rote. It was difficult to take any of it seriously. Around the same time of the tours, hundreds of inmates in New Mexico were suing the state and the privately contracted firm Corizon Health for gross negligence. And it was not only New Mexico. Riots were or had occurred in every region of the nation; they'd struck the California Correctional Center in Susanville, the Tecumseh State Correctional Institution in Nebraska, the Souza-Baranowski Correctional Facility in Boston, the Vaughn Correctional Center in Dover, Delaware; at Pelican Bay; at the El Dorado Correctional Facility in Kansas; at Kinross in Chippewa County, Michigan; at Red Rock in Elroy, Arizona; and at the Lee Correctional Institution in South Carolina—a rampage in which seven inmates were killed and twenty more were injured. Each incident had seen an escalation in violence from the previous, but the causes cited for the riots were the same: "dangerously overcrowded, critically understaffed, and poorly managed" facilities. As for Gregg Marcantel, the opening of the old facility to the public was only the first in a series of spectacles. Later he allowed A&E near-complete discretion while filming the show *Rookie Year*. He followed with a publicity stunt in which he disguised himself and spent forty-eight hours in an administrative segregation unit. He retired in 2016, the public and some politicians viewing his interest in the media to prioritize his celebrity over the day-to-day operations of the dangerous institution.

Eventually, our tour group was escorted to a gift shop. Shot glasses, homemade tortilla rollers. I purchased a size large Old Main T-shirt. On it, an inmate in Ray-Bans opens a prison-issued denim shirt, revealing not his heart but the correctional institution itself. While paying, I overheard one of the women from Durango ask our guide about future plans to clean the museum up. Cory corrected her. "This isn't a museum," he said with a sly smile. "If it were a museum, everything would have to change."

ACKNOWLEDGMENTS

My interest in this story began early, listening to my grandmother, Janell Whitlock (who served for decades as a municipal judge in Carlsbad), and my aunt Cindy (a chief classification officer at the men's facility in Las Cruces) swap tales from the world of criminology that were both frightening and irresistibly engaging to a six-year-old. Without them, this book would never have entered the world. My mother was there, too. Always. She still is. Along with my father, Allen, and my sister, Allison, my family remain the bedrock of matters much larger and more important than writing. Thank you to my extended family: the Sharifs and the Brininstool pack; to Lisa and Reed Crafton, to George Fuller. Thank you to Tommy Crafton and to Roxie Jean Smith—both of whom were immense storytellers in their own right.

This book also could not have been written without the help of journalists, attorneys, archivists, and complete strangers willing to chat with me: Peter Katel, Dan Boyd, Phaedra Haywood, Anne Pederson, John Gaffney, Mark Donatelli, Garvin Isaacs, Dick Blenden, Tom Cherryhomes, Don Stout, and Paul Bohannon; to Carlos Martinez and to Marcella Armijo; to Janet Perkins, and to Mahlon Perkins for his time on the phone with me. Thank you to Alex Tomlin at the New Mexico Corrections Department during my early research, and to Rachel Adler.

I owe a debt of gratitude to the National Endowment for the Arts for seeing something in this project early on: to Amy Stolls, Lan Samantha Chang, Brian Evenson, Dagoberto Gilb, Alyson Hagy, and Hans Weyandt—I'm forever grateful. Thank you to Sacha Idell. Thank you to Wes Enzinna and to Jacob Gross. I'm grateful to the *Southern Review* and to *VICE*, in which excerpts from this book first appeared.

Thank you to the Inprint Foundation and to the creative writing program at the University of Houston. Enormous shout-out to Glenn Shaheen and Laurie Ann Cedilnik.

I'd assumed the story of what happened in Santa Fe in 1980 was widely known. It wasn't until a back-patio chat with a colleague and a true friend and, frankly, the most brilliant mind in academe, Michael J. Martin (he conscripted me into writing this) that I recognized value in pursuing this project. Michael was encouraging all along despite seeing the absolute worst of times. Thank you to John A. McDermott and to Christine Butterworth-McDermott: the opportunities you have offered me have been tremendous. The same can be said to Billie Longino, a real talent and a superb conversationalist. Much gratitude to Tyrone Jaeger for having me out to Hendrix College, and to Daryl Farmer for having me Zoom in to the University of Alaska–Fairbanks.

I am lucky to have Jody Kahn as an agent. She believed in this project early, was unflagging in that belief, and was a champion for the work. You're the best.

It was an honor to work with James McCoy at the University of Iowa Press. His revisions were wise and his sense of humor during our phone calls helped with what was an otherwise grim subject matter. He's also the best reader I've ever met.

Finally, to Chelsea: the thousands of miles, the dingy motels, the court clerks offices and bad coffee, the research support. But, more importantly, being there. Being here. I only know to say thank you.